San Diego Cooks

LIGAYA MALONES

photography by

DEANNA SANDOVAL

San Diego Cooks

Recipes from the Region's Favorite Eateries, Bakeries, and Bars

Figure 1
Vancouver / Toronto / Berkeley

For San Diego's chefs, restaurateurs, soil whisperers, sea people, food purveyors, beverage makers, and other talented folks who keep us nourished and connected beyond the palate.

Cataloguing data is available from Library and Archives Canada

ISBN 978-1-77327-246-7 (hbk.)

Design by Naomi MacDougall and Jessica Sullivan | DSGN Dept.
Photography by Deanna Sandoval
Food and props styling by Taylor Chloe Berk
Photography assistance by Keith Lord
Ligaya Malones and Deanna Sandoval photo by Jim Sullivan
Editing by Michelle Meade
Copy editing by Pam Robertson
Proofreading by Breanne MacDonald
Indexing by Iva Cheung

Printed and bound in China by Shenzhen Reliance Printing Co., Ltd.

Figure 1 Publishing Inc.
Vancouver BC Canada
www.figure1publishing.com

Figure 1 Publishing works in the traditional, unceded territory of the xʷməθkʷəy̓əm (Musqueam), Sḵwx̱wú7mesh (Squamish), and səlilwətaɬ (Tsleil-Waututh) peoples.

Contents

Introduction

WHEN ONE THINKS OF San Diego's abundance, it's borderline obscene. Miles of frothy coastline, framed by time-etched sandstone bluffs? Check. Proximity to verdant hills, mountains, grasslands, and wildflower-strewn deserts? We've got that too. Near-perpetual sunshine? Yep. Globally inflected dishes that reflect our region's closeness to the sea and to Mexico, and the diversity of its population? Certainly. A superlative restaurant scene? Absolutely.

Within its Pacific waters, enterprising sea wranglers reel in fish, prawns, oysters, and seaweed. Inland, our ranchers rear grass-fed beef and pork and produce free-range eggs. With more farms than any other county in the United States, our farmers, from Valley Center to Rancho Santa Fe, coax the earth to provide San Diegans—and many local chefs—with fresh produce from our own "backyard." And while our neighbors in other parts of the country don insulating layers come fall and winter, San Diegans continue to reap these peak flavors year-round, at home and within our favorite restaurants. "We're working ahead of anyone else in the country as far as seasonality," Pierre Albaladejo, executive chef of Ponto Lago (page 124), says. "That's a big asset for a chef."

Observers of San Diego's restaurant scene, myself included, have witnessed our fine city and its surrounds (which I've called home and reported on for a decade) eclipse its rather flat reputation as a tacos and beer town. To be clear, San Diego slings excellent tacos and beer. The city is also widely regarded as a catalyst for the nationwide craft beer explosion that began in the late 1990s. Not to mention the wines made in the hilly pockets of Escondido and Ramona, and the artisanal spirits and other fermented beverages that dot our urban and suburban landscapes.

Navigating the intricate terrain of San Diego's eats and sips could begin with the city's distinct neighborhoods, including Little Italy, North Park, and Mission Hills. It's worth venturing around the county, too, from Oceanside to Chula Vista. You can also embark on a culinary expedition through a genre of cuisine. One might seek out Barrio Logan for Mexican street food, venture to City Heights for Somali or Ethiopian specialties, or journey further inland to El Cajon, where Middle Eastern restaurants pepper Main Street and serve traditional dishes from Iraq, Lebanon, and Syria. In the heart of San Diego County, buttressed against a military base and crammed between car dealerships, the Convoy District teems with Korean BBQ, Chinese dim sum, Japanese ramen, and much, much more.

You'll also find Michelin-starred and -recognized establishments, including Valle (page 166) in Oceanside. Yet local culinary talent and passion is everywhere. They're plating up vegetarian chilaquiles-stuffed tortas alongside fresh fruits and veggies at the farmers' market. They're firing up scratch-made pizzas in the middle of a beer garden that's wedged in an industrial park (page 120). They are tucked into an odd corner of Downtown, engulfed by a ballpark and apartments, and serving succulent Aleppo-chili-rubbed chicken to reignite our enthusiasm for poultry. In our county's most northern coastal parts, they are thriving with a plant-based menu and generating little waste in the process. And in an innocuous shopping mall in our eastern suburbs, they're churning out flaky and rich vegan pastries (page 148).

And lucky for us, some of these beloved restaurants and bakeries are pulling back the curtain on their most iconic dishes and drinks for us to recreate at home. If you've had a pulse on our evolving, ingredient-driven culinary community, you'll notice some familiar dishes, like JRDN's Steamed Mussels (page 65) and Glass Box's Taiwanese Beef Noodle Soup (page 60).

Some recipes come together relatively quickly with a quick sear of protein and few turns of a mixing bowl, like TJ Oyster Bar's Baja Fish Tacos (page 164) and Kettner Exchange's Kale Salad with Lemon-Pepper Dressing (page 69). Others are ideal for crowds, like Smokin J's Smoked Brisket Chili with Cornbread (page 147), and Extraordinary Desserts's Lemon Meringue Cake (page 52). And a few recipes, like Valle's Onion Tart (page 170) and AVANT's Grilled Steak with Mole Demi and Guajillo Marmalade (page 36), may require sourcing more ingredients and learning unpracticed techniques, and will challenge adventurous home cooks.

For those newer to or reacquainting themselves with San Diego's culinary diversity, these recipes demonstrate that things are looking a little (well, a lot) different these days. Welcome to a taste of some of the chefs, bakers, distillers, and more who are nourishing us with their passion, stories, eats, and sips throughout our dynamic region.

The Restaurants

The Recipes

The Recipes

San Diego Cooks

24 SUNS

▶ *SAN DIEGO* ◀

CHEF (L) Nicholas Webber
CHEF (R) Jacob Jordan

FOR LONGTIME southern Californian chefs Nicholas Webber and Jacob Jordan, discovery and creativity go hand in hand. Their menus journey through their French and Italian culinary training, an intense exploration of regional Chinese cuisine, and the bounty of San Diego's local growers and purveyors. As fine-dining alums who met on the canapé station at three-Michelin-starred Addison in Carmel Valley, 24 Suns is their first solo project.

Their brick-and-mortar concept was born from their pop-up dim sum experience, and its earliest iterations began casually enough—just a dinner party among people they knew. They kept making dumplings and needed more people to help eat them. "It started out as friends, then friends of friends, then next thing you know we have sixteen people we don't know in my backyard," Jordan says.

They've been serving elevated mashups that stretch their training and interests to their limits since 2021. Take their "putta'nut'sca," for example: a vegan nut braise that cooks for days in tomato sauce with capers, olive brine, and chili oil and is served over Chinese egg noodles. "It straddles that line: is it an Italian or a Chinese experience? It's neither, it's just us," Webber says.

Both champion the satisfaction that comes with rigorous historical and cultural research to challenge San Diego's palates—like serving a bit of chewy, toothsome jellyfish as an amuse-bouche. "The food also has our French influence, so it's important for us to know the cultural background. This way, we're not diluting anything," Webber says.

JIAOZI WRAPPERS

¾ cup all-purpose flour,
 plus extra for dusting

¾ cup bread flour

SCALLOP AND PORK FILLING

8 to 10 diver scallops,
finely chopped

½ lb ground pork

2 bunches chives, finely chopped

3 cloves garlic, finely chopped

2 Tbsp mirin

2 Tbsp soy sauce

1 Tbsp rice wine vinegar

2 tsp salt

1 tsp sesame oil

1 tsp white pepper

1 tsp MSG

DOUBANJIANG BUTTER SAUCE

½ cup (1 stick) + 1 Tbsp cold butter
(divided)

2 shallots, thinly sliced

4 cloves garlic, thinly sliced

3 Tbsp fermented bean paste
(doubanjiang)

½ cup white wine

½ cup heavy cream

1 Tbsp mirin

2 tsp salt

1 tsp MSG

Juice of ½ lemon

Scallop and Pork Jiaozi with Doubanjiang Butter Sauce

SERVES
4–6

"*Jiaozi* are classic Chinese dumplings. We impart our traditional French training to the sauce work and, by combining two techniques, we create something new. *Doubanjiang* is a powerful and aromatic fermented broad bean paste and a quintessential Sichuan flavor. The fragrant spice pairs beautifully with the freshest scallops you can find."

Jiaozi wrappers can be made a day ahead. In a pinch, store-bought gyoza wrappers make an acceptable substitute.

Jiaozi wrappers Combine both flours in a large bowl and whisk. Add ¼ cup of warm water (around 100°F) and mix with a spatula until absorbed. Add 2½ tablespoons of room-temperature water and mix until small clumps of dough form. Knead in the bowl for 5 minutes, or until a shaggy dough starts to form. Cover dough with a dish towel and set aside to rest for 10 minutes.

Turn dough onto a floured surface and knead for 15 minutes, until smooth. (Alternatively, mix in a stand mixer fitted with the hook attachment for 10 minutes.) If dough is too wet, add a tablespoon of flour at a time while kneading. Wrap in plastic wrap and refrigerate at least 45 minutes or overnight.

Scallop and pork filling In a bowl, combine scallops, pork, chives, and garlic.

Combine the remaining ingredients in a separate bowl and mix well. Add the seasoning to the pork mixture and gently combine. Be careful not to overmix; otherwise, the filling toughens when cooked. Cover in plastic wrap and chill in the refrigerator until completely cool.

Doubanjiang butter sauce Heat 1 tablespoon of butter in a large skillet over low heat. Add shallots and garlic and sauté for 4 minutes, until translucent. Stir in doubanjiang.

Add wine, reduce heat to medium, and simmer for 5 minutes, or until reduced by half. Add cream and cook for another 8 minutes, or

until reduced by half and thickened. Add the remaining ½ cup (1 stick) cold butter, 1 tablespoon at a time, whisking continuously until incorporated. Stir in the remaining ingredients and adjust seasoning to taste.

Strain sauce through a fine-mesh sieve.

Assembly Divide dough into 4 equal portions. Using a rolling pin, flatten them until they're thin enough for a pasta roller. Flour dough generously, then pass a portion through the roller. Repeat, changing to a thinner setting each time, until the dough is translucent. Repeat with the remaining portions. Using a 2-inch ring mold, punch out 20 circles. Place the wrappers on a plate, separating them with parchment paper to prevent them from sticking.

Place 1 tablespoon of filling in the center of each wrapper. Fold in half without sealing. Working from one side of the opening, pinch ½ inch of dough together then fold one piece of the wrapper over itself again at ½-inch intervals, pinching and crimping. Keep the wrap close to

the filling to avoid air pockets. Repeat, working along the open edge, until the dumpling is completely sealed. Repeat with the remaining wrappers and filling. Place the dumplings in a bamboo steamer.

Steam dumplings for 5 minutes, until hot in the center and fully cooked. Transfer to a serving plate and generously cover with doubanjiang butter sauce. Garnish with sliced chives.

1 cup fermented black beans
(see Note)

⅓ cup mirin

1 Tbsp soy sauce

1 (2-lb) rack of lamb

1 quantity Fermented
  Black Bean Cure (see here)

⅔ cup mint leaves,
  for garnish

1 cup mirin

2 Tbsp Dijon mustard

2 Tbsp grated ginger

4 tsp salt

6 peaches, pitted and quartered

Fermented Black Bean Smoked Lamb Chops

SERVES
6–8

"This dish is inspired by the regional cuisine of northern China, where they grow wheat and other grains over rice in their grasslands and raise grazing animals such as lamb. It combines salty black bean, earthy and savory lamb, and sweet peaches."

Fermented black bean cure Whisk all ingredients in a mixing bowl, then set aside.

Lamb chops Using gloved hands, thoroughly coat lamb rack in the fermented black bean cure. Place lamb on a rack over a baking sheet, leave uncovered, and cure in the refrigerator for 24 hours.

Set your smoker to 200°F. Wipe away excess cure. Place a small metal dish or pan of water in the smoker to maintain moisture. Place lamb on a wire rack and set into the preheated smoker. Smoke for 1 hour to 1 hour and 20 minutes, rotating once halfway through, or until a probe thermometer reads 130°F. Transfer to a cutting board and set aside to rest for at least 25 minutes.

Ginger peaches In a medium bowl, combine mirin, mustard, ginger, and salt. Place peaches into the marinade and gently mix. Refrigerate for 30 minutes to marinate.

Preheat a grill over high heat. Add peaches and grill on each side until lightly charred. (Alternatively, grill peaches in a cast-iron pan over medium-high heat.) Return peaches to the marinade.

Assembly Heat a large skillet over medium-high heat. Add lamb racks and sear for 3 to 5 minutes on each side, until browned and warm throughout.

Slice lamb chops between the bones and arrange on a serving platter. Remove peaches from the marinade and arrange them on the platter. Garnish with mint.

NOTE *Fermented black beans are black soybeans that have been fermented with salt. Savory and slightly pungent, they are widely used in China to add umami to regional dishes. They can be purchased at Asian grocers.*

264 FRESCO

▶ *CARLSBAD* ◀

CHEF (L) Enrique Dela Paz
OWNER (C) Linda DiNitto
CHEF (R) Nicholas Vasquez

264 FRESCO is a charming seaside Italian restaurant in Carlsbad, offering a vibrant and welcoming dining experience both inside and out. The wood-fired pizza oven is nestled in a corner of its outdoor patio; the spacious dining rooms lined with lime green banquettes seat small and large groups; and a chic adults-only, open-air bar and lounge on its upper deck is prime sunset viewing. Guests favor the generously portioned lasagna, layered with bolognese, béchamel, and fresh tomatoes, as well as the comforting baked rigatoni with Italian sausage, Parmesan, and mozzarella.

Enrique Dela Paz assumed the executive chef role in 2022, following his time as executive sous chef of Cucina Enoteca in Del Mar. For more than two decades, owner Linda DiNitto has channeled a passion for sharing her Italian culture through food and gathering with friends and family via 264 Fresco.

In 2024, Nicholas Vasquez, an Urban Solace alum, took over as executive chef. At 264 Fresco, Vasquez aims to "create great food and a memorable experience, in an environment in which people are excited to come to work and grow with the people [they] get the opportunity to work with everyday." It takes patience and finesse to offer a menu that suits the tastes and expectations of the full spectrum of guests, from nearby beachgoers to those who've planned for an evening of wining and dining, and Vasquez is up for the task. "My restaurants reflect my culture and experiences. It is food that I grew up eating and that my family still enjoys," DiNitto says.

▶ *264 Lasagna and Noci Salad*

APPLE CIDER VINAIGRETTE

½ Tbsp whole grain mustard

2 Tbsp apple juice

2 Tbsp apple cider vinegar

1 Tbsp honey

½ tsp thyme leaves

1 cup extra-virgin olive oil

Salt, to taste

SALAD

1 lb spring mix greens

2 Granny Smith apples, cored and sliced

¾ cup dried cranberries

¾ cup crumbled Gorgonzola cheese

¾ cup candied or regular walnuts

Noci Salad

SERVES
6

Apple cider vinaigrette Combine all ingredients, except oil and salt, in a blender and blend. Slowly add oil and blend until emulsified to desired consistency. Season with salt to taste.

Leftover dressing can be stored in an airtight container for 3 to 4 days.

Salad In a large bowl, combine all ingredients.

Assembly Drizzle ½ cup of vinaigrette over the salad and toss gently. Taste and add more dressing, if desired.

LASAGNA

12 lasagna sheets, uncooked

PORK FILLING

2 Tbsp olive oil

½ lb ground pork

3 cloves garlic, finely chopped

1 large yellow onion, chopped (1 cup)

1 tsp fennel seeds

1 tsp red chili flakes

½ tsp dried oregano

½ tsp paprika

Salt and pepper, to taste

MEAT SAUCE

2 Tbsp olive oil

½ lb ground beef

1 to 2 stalks celery, finely chopped (½ cup)

1 yellow onion, finely chopped (½ cup)

1 carrot, finely chopped (½ cup)

6 to 8 cloves garlic, finely chopped

4½ cups tomato sauce

Salt and pepper, to taste

CHEESE FILLING

4 cups shredded mozzarella

1 cup grated Parmesan

¼ cup finely chopped Italian parsley

¼ cup thinly sliced basil

ASSEMBLY

2 cups ricotta

264 Lasagna

Lasagna Bring a large saucepan of salted water to a boil. Add pasta and cook according to the package directions until al dente. Drain, then rinse under cold running water. Set aside.

Pork filling Heat oil in a large skillet over medium-high heat. Add pork, garlic, and onion and sauté for 7 minutes, or until pork is no longer pink. Add fennel, chili flakes, oregano, and paprika. Season with salt and pepper and sauté for another 5 to 10 minutes, until fully cooked. Set aside.

Meat sauce Heat oil in a large skillet over medium heat. Add beef, celery, onion, carrot, and garlic and sauté for 10 to 12 minutes, until beef is fully cooked and onions are translucent. Drain excess oil. Stir in tomato sauce, then season with salt and pepper. Reduce heat to low and simmer, uncovered, for 10 to 15 minutes, until sauce thickens. Set aside.

Cheese filling Meanwhile, combine all ingredients. Refrigerate until needed.

Assembly Preheat the oven to 350°F.

Ladle a cup of meat sauce into a 9- × 13-inch baking dish and spread out. Top with 3 sheets cooked lasagna. Layer with the pork filling and dollops of ricotta, then top with 1 cup cheese filling and ¼ cup meat sauce. Repeat steps until all lasagna sheets are used. Finish with a final layer of meat sauce. (Set aside the remaining cheese filling for sprinkling on top later.) Cover with aluminum foil and bake for 30 to 45 minutes.

Remove foil and sprinkle with remaining cheese filling. Bake, uncovered, for another 10 minutes, until golden brown. If desired, broil for 2 minutes.

Rest for 10 minutes, then serve.

A.R. VALENTIEN

▶ *LA JOLLA* ◀

CHEF / Kelli Crosson

KELLI CROSSON always knew she wanted to be a chef, though the path to professional kitchens took some twists and turns. Despite Crosson's early love for baking with her family, growing up watching Julia Child on PBS, and tending to her parents' citrus orchard in the Central Valley, it took an attempt at college and a stint in marketing before she made her way to culinary school and into the kitchen for good.

As executive chef of A.R. Valentien at The Lodge at Torrey Pines, Crosson shepherds excellently prepared California-French classics that showcase the region's ingredients at their best—that is, without extensive manipulation. From rotating pâtés to an iconic roast duck to Chicken Under a Brick (a lunchtime favorite), Crosson champions what she calls foundational cooking. "We make everything in-house," Crosson says.

She is also proud of the kitchen's flexibility to make real-time menu adjustments to ensure guests' plates are filled with ingredients at their peak. "Not all restaurants are able to make these in-the-moment changes," Crosson says. And with its Craftsman-style, indoor-outdoor dining room boasting unparalleled oceanscape just beyond the Torrey Pines Golf Course, it's why dining here is a singular San Diego experience.

1 cup + 1 Tbsp olive oil (divided)

4 (4-oz) albacore tuna loins, trimmed into blocks (see Note)

Salt and white pepper, to taste

1 large scallion or ½ yellow onion, thinly sliced

1 small bulb fennel, thinly sliced

6 sweet peppers, such as pimento, Cubanelle, Italian Long, or Jimmy Nardello, thinly sliced with a mandoline

5 cloves garlic, thinly sliced

¼ cup packed brown sugar

2 cups pitted Castelvetrano olives

¼ cup apple cider vinegar

Sea salt, for sprinkling (optional)

Albacore "en Escabeche"

SERVES
4

Heat 1 tablespoon of oil in a skillet over medium-high heat. Season tuna loins with salt and white pepper, then add them to the hot pan and sear for 30 seconds on each side, for rare to medium-rare. Transfer to a deep dish, large enough to fit tuna pieces snugly. Set aside.

Heat ½ cup of oil in a large skillet. Add scallion (or onion) and fennel and sauté for 5 minutes. Add sweet peppers and garlic and sauté for another 2 minutes, until peppers are cooked through but not falling apart. Add brown sugar and stir until dissolved. Stir in olives and vinegar and cook for another 5 minutes until flavors combine. Add the remaining ½ cup of oil.

While still warm, pour the mixture over the seared tuna. Let cool to room temperature, then refrigerate overnight.

Assembly Remove the tuna loins from the refrigerator and set aside for 1 hour. Thinly slice them, then arrange on plates. Spoon escabeche sauce over top. If desired, finish with sea salt.

NOTE Cutting tuna loins into blocks creates a more uniform shape and helps to retain rareness on the inside.

2 cups peeled garlic cloves

GARLIC-LEMON VINAIGRETTE

½ cup Garlic Purée (see here)

¼ cup fresh lemon juice

½ cup olive oil

½ cup grapeseed oil (or other neutral oil you prefer for dressings)

Salt and pepper, to taste

PORK LOIN

¾ cup salt, plus extra to taste

⅔ cup sugar

3 lbs bone-in, Niman Ranch center-cut pork loin

2 heads garlic, halved horizontally

10 sprigs thyme

4 bay leaves

Pepper, to taste

WATERCRESS SALAD

2 bunches watercress

3 small summer squash (any variation of pattypan, yellow, or zucchini will work)

3 Tbsp Garlic-Lemon Vinaigrette (see here)

¼ cup crumbled goat cheese

¼ cup toasted hazelnuts

Salt and pepper, to taste

Smoked Pork Loin with Watercress Salad

SERVES

6

At A.R. Valentien, they serve the pork loin thinly sliced with a salad of watercress, shaved summer squash, toasted hazelnuts, crumbled goat cheese, and garlic-lemon vinaigrette. Roasted vegetables would make an equally delicious accompaniment.

Garlic purée Place garlic cloves in a small pot and cover with an inch of cold water. Bring to a boil, then strain and discard water. Place the garlic back in the pot and repeat the process three more times until the garlic is soft and the sharpness has been removed.

After boiling and straining garlic the fourth and final time, transfer the soft cloves to a blender and purée until smooth. If possible, pass through a fine-mesh sieve. (You can skip this step, but your vinaigrette may be a bit chunky.)

Garlic-lemon vinaigrette Give your blender a quick rinse and add garlic purée and lemon juice. Blend until smooth, then slowly add the oils until emulsified. Season to taste with salt and pepper.

Pork loin In a large stockpot, combine salt, sugar, and 7 quarts of water. Heat over high heat until sugar and salt have dissolved. Set aside to cool completely. Add pork loin, garlic, thyme, and bay leaves. Brine overnight.

Remove pork loin from the brine and dry completely. Season generously with salt and pepper. Start an oakwood fire in a smoker. Let coals burn until they hold a temperature of 350°F. Cook pork for 30 minutes, rotating occasionally to ensure even cooking, until the internal temperature reaches 145°F. Set aside to rest for 10 minutes.

Remove the loin from the bone, then slice.

Watercress salad Trim the long stems of the watercress. Using a mandoline or a sharp knife, thinly slice summer squash lengthwise to create long ribbons. Measure the vinaigrette into a large bowl. Add the watercress, shaved squash, goat cheese, and hazelnuts and toss gently. Season to taste with salt and pepper.

Serve immediately with the smoked pork loin.

AMBROGIO
BY ACQUERELLO

▶ *LA JOLLA* ◀

CHEF / Silvio Salmoiraghi

AMBROGIO BY ACQUERELLO, located in La Jolla and led by chef Silvio Salmoiraghi, invites San Diegans to experience a side of Italian cuisine many (including Italians themselves) aren't typically familiar with. For example, the fine-dining restaurant pays tribute to the traditional Venetian cod and polenta dish with toasted polenta (page 31). It infuses a smoky flavor to the black cod, a beloved San Diegan sea protein, without smoking the fish itself. (Historically, the dish was served as a large, frugal one-pot meal to satiate large families.) And if there is pasta on Ambrogio by Acquerello's eight-course tasting menu, it might arrive to the table as an Italian take on ramen, where goat's curd–filled rigatoni replace long, thin noodles. Or as traditional linguine and Parmigiano-Reggiano served with the modern twist of mint and basil (page 29).

The Ambrogio by Acquerello team— including owners Giacomo Pizzigoni and Andrea Burrone and chef-partner Choi Cheolhyeok— hails from Milan. While they may be thousands of miles away from their native Italy, they don't see many differences between the two cities when it comes to cuisine. Both locales are surrounded by water, fresh produce, and specialty products and share a border with other cultures. During Ambrogio by Acquerello's developmental days, "We were trying to use pure Italian ingredients," Pizzigoni says, "until we looked at it the other way around and incorporated local ingredients and tastes into Chef's philosophy." Salmoiraghi's deft command of flavors and techniques draws on thirty years of cooking and globetrotting— from France to Japan, Korea to Ireland—and an expansive perspective. "Italian cuisine," Salmoiraghi explains, "is a state of mind with an artistic approach to putting ingredients together. At Acquerello, we believe that it matters not what you cook, but how and why you cook it."

LEMON DRESSING

4 to 5 lemons, peeled and sliced

Pinch of fine salt

Extra-virgin olive oil, for drizzling

LINGUINE

¾ cup + 2 tsp (1¾ sticks) butter

20 mint leaves (divided)

11 oz linguine

6 basil leaves, thinly sliced

2 tsp lemon juice

1½ cups grated Parmigiano-Reggiano, preferably aged 24 months

Linguine with Parmesan and Mint (*Linguine Parmigiano e Menta*)

SERVES 4

This heritage recipe marries contemporary flair with the nostalgia of Silvio Salmoiraghi's beloved childhood flavors. The combination of linguine, aged Parmigiano-Reggiano, and fresh mint and basil transports you to Italy's sun-soaked landscapes.

Lemon dressing Combine all ingredients in a medium saucepan and cook over low heat for 20 minutes, until reduced to a soft compote. Strain.

Linguine Melt the butter in a small saucepan over medium-low heat.

Meanwhile, in a small skillet, fry 4 mint leaves over medium to high heat for a few seconds, until they become translucent. Set aside.

Bring a large saucepan of salted water to a boil. Add pasta and cook according to the package directions or for 8 to 10 minutes, just before it turns al dente. Drain, reserving a cup of pasta water.

In a large skillet, combine linguine, three-quarters of the melted butter, and some of the pasta water. Cook for a minute over medium heat, until al dente.

Stir in the remaining butter, fresh mint, basil, and lemon juice. Add Parmigiano-Reggiano and mix until saucy. If needed, add a little more pasta water.

Place a dollop of lemon dressing in the center of each plate. Arrange a nest of pasta on top. Top with the remaining sauce and garnish with crumbled fried mint.

BLACK COD

1 (14-oz) skin-on, boneless black cod fillet

GRUYÈRE SAUCE

2½ tsp butter
1½ Tbsp "00" flour
½ cup milk
½ cup heavy cream
¼ cup grated Gruyère cheese
½ Tbsp Dijon mustard
Salt, to taste

PARSLEY SAUCE

¾ cup chopped Italian parsley
½ teaspoon wasabi paste
3 Tbsp extra-virgin olive oil
Salt, to taste

POLENTA

¾ cup polenta
Pinch of salt
3½ Tbsp butter
2 tsp lemon juice

ASSEMBLY

Salt, to taste
5 to 6 sprigs Italian parsley, for garnish
Grated zest of 1 lemon, for garnish

Black Cod and Polenta
(*Merluzzo e Polenta*)

SERVES
4

This historical dish embraces Italy's inland and coastal regions through a century-old Venetian marriage of creamy polenta with savory, umami-boasting black cod. Ambrogio by Acquerello's version features crispy cod with a velvety Gruyère sauce, contemporized by toasted polenta and a parsley-wasabi sauce. Best enjoyed al fresco, as they do in Italy.

Black cod Portion cod into 4 equal pieces. Pat dry and refrigerate.

Gruyère sauce Melt butter in a saucepan over medium heat. Stir in flour and lightly cook for 5 minutes, until nutty and golden. (Do not brown.) Pour in milk and cream and gently simmer for 5 to 7 minutes, stirring occasionally, until thickened to a sauce. Remove from heat.

Whisk in cheese and mustard, then season to taste with salt. Place plastic wrap directly on the surface to prevent a skin from forming. Set aside and keep warm until needed.

Parsley sauce Fill a bowl with ice water. Bring a small saucepan of salted water to a boil. Add parsley and cook for 5 minutes. Using a slotted spoon, immediately transfer parsley to the bowl of ice water. Reserve the cooking water.

In a blender, combine parsley, wasabi, oil, and enough cooking water to make a sauce thick enough to coat the back of a spoon. Season to taste with salt. Set sauce aside until needed.

Polenta Combine polenta and salt in a small skillet and toast over medium heat. Add butter and cook until melted. Stir in lemon juice. Set aside.

Assembly Preheat oven to broil.

Heat a large skillet over high heat. Season the black cod with salt, then add it to the skillet, skin side down, until skin is crispy. Transfer seared cod to a baking sheet, skin side up, and broil for 2 minutes.

Place 2 tablespoons of warm Gruyère sauce in the center of each plate. Place a piece of cod on top, skin side up. Spoon parsley sauce along one side of the plate, creating a half-moon shape.

Heat the polenta vigorously until the butter starts to foam. Add the fluffy polenta to each plate (about 3 tablespoons), then garnish with parsley and lemon zest atop the cod.

Serve immediately.

AVANT

▶ *RANCHO BERNARDO* ◀

CHEF / Sergio Jimenez

SERGIO JIMENEZ'S presence at AVANT at Rancho Bernardo Inn is a homecoming. Returning as chef de cuisine, Jimenez started as the restaurant's sauté cook in 2014. It was always his goal to take over one day, even as he pursued other professional opportunities in the years between. At AVANT, Jimenez leads a team crafting a dinner menu of classic dishes with a Baja California twist and utilizes produce and herbs like purslane and sorrel from the onsite chef's garden. The restaurant's oversized, crescent-shaped booths, sumptuous dark leather seats, and fireplace set the tone for a menu meant to be shared, family-style, like a tower of oysters, prawns, and other seafood selections, and larger plates with sides to pass around, such as charred broccoli rabe with citrus salsa. AVANT's most requested dish of the moment is their Rosewood Wagyu rib eye cap, which Jimenez wraps into a spiral, sears, and pairs with black garlic demi-glace. The signature dish also includes charred, herb-crusted potatoes and guajillo marmalade—at once sweet, smoky, and spicy. "It's my take on a loaded American baked potato," Jimenez says. A born and raised San Diegan, Jimenez spent much of his culinary career in the region. Growing up, he often helped his aunt and mom at the taco stand they'd set up in the driveway every weekend. People snaked around the block while Jimenez bussed tables. It was then that Jimenez first internalized that food and taking care of people are inextricable, and that passion and love are necessary ingredients in the kitchen.

▶ *Grilled Steak with Mole Demi and Guajillo Marmalade*

WHIPPED CRÈME FRAÎCHE

4 cups heavy whipping cream

2 cups buttermilk

2 Tbsp extra-hot horseradish, such as Atomic

1 Tbsp salt

CLOVER LEAF ROLLS

2 cups bread flour, plus extra for dusting

2 Tbsp salt

2½ cups warm milk

⅓ cup sugar

1.2 oz dry yeast

¾ cup + 2½ tsp butter (1¾ sticks + ½ tsp), room temperature, plus extra for greasing and brushing

2 eggs

Clover Leaf Rolls with Whipped Crème Fraîche and Everything Seasoning

MAKES
4 rolls

Shaped like the eponymous plant, these fluffy rolls are paired with horseradish crème fraîche and garnished with everything seasoning—a mix of sesame, fennel seeds, caraway seeds, and garlic.

If you're short on time, you can use store-bought crème fraîche.

Whipped crème fraîche Combine cream and buttermilk in a bowl. Partially cover and set in the fridge to rest for 72 hours.

Line a baking tray with pieces of cheesecloth, allowing them to overlap and hang over the edges. Pour the cream mixture onto the prepared baking tray, then cover the mixture with more cheesecloth and fold the edges over to encase the fermented cream and soak up excess liquid. Wrap the entire tray in plastic wrap. Refrigerate for 24 hours, until thickened to desired consistency.

In a mixer, combine 4 cups crème fraiche, horseradish, and salt. Whisk for 5 minutes at medium speed, until light and airy.

Clover leaf rolls In the bowl of a stand mixer fitted with the paddle attachment, combine flour and salt and set aside.

In a separate bowl, combine milk, sugar, and yeast. Set aside in the warmest part of the kitchen for 45 minutes.

Mix the flour at medium speed, gradually incorporating butter (reserving 4 teaspoons for the muffin tin) and eggs until fully combined. Pour in milk, 1 cup at a time, then mix dough for 5 minutes at low speed, until dough is sticky but pulls away easily from the bowl. Grease another bowl, then add the dough. Set aside to rest for 10 to 20 minutes, until doubled in size.

EVERYTHING SEASONING

2 Tbsp white sesame seeds

2 Tbsp black sesame seeds

2 Tbsp onion flakes or onion powder

2 tsp sea salt

1 tsp granulated garlic

1 tsp caraway seeds

1 tsp fennel seeds

1 tsp sugar

Add 1 teaspoon of the reserved butter into each large cup of a four-cup muffin tin. Place the dough ball on a clean, lightly floured surface and poke it so it slightly deflates. Using your hands, form 12 balls of dough, about 1 inch in diameter. Add 3 dough balls per cup and set aside to proof in a warm environment for 15 minutes.

Preheat oven to 350°F. Brush rolls with warm butter, then bake for 25 minutes, or until rolls are golden brown. Brush with more warm butter to finish.

Everything seasoning Combine all ingredients in a bowl.

Assembly Sprinkle seasoning over the warm clover rolls. Serve with whipped crème fraîche.

LEEK AND FENNEL ASH

3 bunches fennel tops

3 bunches leek tops

2 tsp garlic powder

2 tsp onion powder

2 tsp smoked paprika

1 tsp sugar

POTATOES

3 lbs fingerling potatoes

1 cup salt

2 Tbsp Leek and Fennel Ash (see here)

1 tsp paprika

MOLE DEMI

2 qts veal or beef stock

½ cup lard or cooking oil (divided)

1½ lbs bone marrow

5 cloves garlic

4 pasilla chiles

½ cup pine nuts

2 Tbsp banana chips

1 star anise

2 whole cloves

1 Tbsp black peppercorns

½ Tbsp cumin seeds

½ Tbsp oregano

½ Tbsp coriander seeds

1 onion, chopped

1 Tbsp tomato paste

½ slice white bread

3 (6-inch) corn tortillas

2 Tbsp white sesame seeds

2 Tbsp raisins

2 Tbsp brown sugar

¼ wheel Abuelita chocolate (see Note)

Salt and pepper, to taste

Lemon juice, to taste

Grilled Steak with Mole Demi and Guajillo Marmalade

Chef Sergio Jimenez draws on his Mexican heritage to up the interest in a classic steak and potato dish with a long-simmered mole sauce and a guajillo chile marmalade spiced with cumin and sumac.

Leek and fennel ash (see Note) Preheat oven to 400°F. Spread out fennel and leek tops on a baking sheet in a single layer. Bake for 1½ hours, until dried, dark, and caramelized. Transfer to a blender or food processor and blend to a powder. Place the powder in a small bowl, then stir in the remaining ingredients.

NOTE Leftover ash may be stored in an airtight container with a silica packet, in a cool, dry place, for up to 12 months. Without the silica packet, ash will keep for up to 6 months.

Potatoes Place potatoes in a large saucepan. Cover with water, then add the salt. Boil for 30 minutes, until potatoes can be easily pierced with a fork. Drain most of the water, leaving enough to cover the bottom of the pan. Sprinkle in ash and paprika and gently shake the pot to mix, and so potatoes don't stick to the bottom. Cook potatoes for another 3 to 5 minutes over medium-low heat until the water evaporates. Strain and air dry.

Mole demi Simmer stock in a stockpot for 20 to 45 minutes, until reduced by half.

Heat at least ¼ cup of lard (or oil) in a separate saucepan over medium-low heat, taking care not to burn. Add bone marrow and fry for 2 to 3 minutes, until charred and caramelized. Using tongs, transfer marrow to a large plate. Repeat with the garlic and then the chiles, separately, until charred. Repeat with pine nuts and banana chips, adding a little more lard (or oil) as needed.

GUAJILLO MARMALADE

2 Tbsp grapeseed oil, or beef fat if available

1 lb beef trim

3 dried guajillo chiles

1 onion, chopped

1 carrot, chopped

5 cloves garlic, sliced

¼ cup sugar

1 Tbsp ground cumin

4 cups veal stock

1 cup red wine

1 cup red wine vinegar

1 cup (2 sticks) butter

2 Tbsp ground sumac

1 Tbsp golden raisins

1 tsp pectin

Salt, to taste

GRILLED STEAK

4 to 6 (6-oz) Wagyu striploin steaks

Salt and pepper, to taste

ASSEMBLY

Flaky finishing salt, for garnish

Sprig of oregano, leaves minced

Nasturtium leaves, for garnish (optional)

Then toast the spices until fragrant. Caramelize the onion, adding the tomato paste once onion begins to soften. Toast the slice of bread and tortillas in the same pan.

In a blender, combine the charred and caramelized ingredients, the toasted bread and tortillas, and the warm stock. Add the pine nuts, banana chips, sesame seeds, raisins, brown sugar, and the toasted spices and blend until smooth. Transfer mixture to a large saucepan. Bring to a boil, then reduce heat to medium-low and simmer, partially covered, for 1 hour, or until reduced by half. Grate in chocolate.

Pour in 4 cups of water and simmer for another hour, until reduced by half. Season to taste with salt and pepper and add a squeeze of lemon juice to finish.

NOTE *Abuelita chocolate is available in disks that can be snapped into wedges for your desired amount.*

Guajillo marmalade   Heat oil (or beef fat) in a large stockpot over medium-high heat. Add beef trim, then add chiles, onion, carrot, and garlic and sauté for 10 to 15 minutes, until caramelized. Add sugar and cumin and cook for another 20 minutes.

Pour in stock, wine, and vinegar. Cook for at least 1 hour, until beef is soft. Stir in butter, sumac, raisins, and pectin. Season to taste with salt.

Grilled steak   Preheat a grill over medium-high heat. Season steaks with salt and pepper. Add steaks to the grill and cook for 3 minutes on each side. Set aside for 5 minutes.

Assembly   Once steaks have rested, place 2 tablespoons of mole demi in the center of each plate and place steak next to it. Garnish steak with flaky salt. Place 3 to 4 potatoes on the side, then spoon a tablespoon of guajillo marmalade over the potatoes and garnish with minced oregano and nasturtium leaves (if using).

CASA OCHO

▶ *SAN DIEGO* ◀

CHEFS / Ana Ochoa
and Chris Casas

MEXICAN FOOD is an intrinsic part of San Diego's food scene. Among the ubiquitous carne asada burritos and fish tacos, Casa Ocho is redefining—or, better yet, expanding—our understanding of Mexican food in America's Finest City. Married duo Ana Ochoa and Chris Casas combine flavors and textures of their cross-border upbringings in a tightly edited menu of vegetarian dishes like tortas, quesadillas, and chilaquiles. One of their signature items, their favorite childhood breakfast dish, has chilaquiles stuffed into a torta with soy-based chorizo and a cilantro crema that mimics the lusciousness of avocado yet instead involves sour cream, zucchini, tomatillos, and garlic. "It's Mexican food, and it's grubby," Ochoa says. It's an ode to Tijuana street-food culture—and they call it "Mexa Grub."

Growing up in Tijuana, a typical week included frequenting their favorite street-food vendors and eating traditional home-cooked meals, as well as crossing the border into San Diego for school and weekend shopping and dining. After working through the ranks of different hospitality jobs over the years, they combined their collective experiences, applied them toward their own concept in 2020, and marked a return to their roots. "We're border kids," Casas says. "We're half from there, half from here. We've been connected to the city since we were born." Currently, Casa Ocho operates as a weekly pop-up around the county but there is a brick-and-mortar space coming soon.

▶ *La Torta del Ocho and Salsa Verde*

2 cups tomato sauce (see Note)

1 tsp canola oil

2 cups vegetarian refried beans

1 cup soy-based chorizo, such as Soyrizo

6 telera rolls, halved

Chipotle aioli

Shredded Monterey Jack

2 cups tortilla chips, plus extra for topping

Cilantro crema

Bunch of cilantro, finely chopped

Salsa Verde (page 41), to serve

NOTE *Regular tomato sauce will do, but the chefs recommend combining one part tomato sauce with one part El Pato hot tomato sauce (the one in the yellow can!).*

La Torta del Ocho

"This sandwich was born from our late-night adventures in our early twenties when we used to roam Tijuana's streets in search of the perfect midnight grub," says Ana Ochoa. "It is inspired by our favorite dishes from the countless taco stands, food trucks, and holes-in-the-wall we've frequented over the years."

From its name (a reference to the classic Mexican TV comedy series *El Chavo del Ocho*) to its inception, La Torta del Ocho is an ode to Ochoa and Casas's youth and reminds them to prepare their taste buds for anything.

Telera rolls, cilantro crema, and chipotle aioli can be found at your local panadería and Mexican supermarkets.

Torta Heat tomato sauce in a saucepan over medium heat, stirring frequently, until hot. Set aside.

Heat oil in a small skillet over medium heat. Add refried beans and heat for 5 minutes, folding occasionally, until warmed through. Set aside.

Cook soy-based chorizo in a separate small skillet over high heat for 4 minutes, until browned.

Set the telera rolls out on a cutting board and spread chipotle aioli over the cut sides.

Place each half of one roll on a grill pan, cut side down, and grill over medium-low heat until golden brown.

Using a spatula, carefully flip the bottom half of the roll. Top with refried beans, ensuring the toasted surface is covered. Sprinkle with cheese and grill until it begins to melt. Top with the cooked chorizo.

Flip the top half of the roll and grill until golden brown.

Heat a medium skillet over low heat. Add tortilla chips and your desired amount of tomato sauce on top. Toss together in the pan until chips are fully coated in sauce. Place a few chips atop the chorizo on the bottom half.

Add cilantro crema and cilantro. Drizzle with more chipotle aioli and complete with the top half of the roll. Using a metal spatula, carefully remove your finished torta from the heat and serve immediately with a side of salsa verde. Repeat with the other tortas.

Leftover sandwiches can be stored in the refrigerator for a day. When ready to serve, reheat in a toaster oven or air fryer.

3 tomatillos, husks removed and washed

1 zucchini, sliced

1 clove garlic

2 Tbsp vegetable oil

1 jalapeño, stemmed and halved lengthwise

1 serrano pepper, stemmed and halved lengthwise

½ bunch cilantro, stems removed

Salt, to taste

Salsa Verde

This versatile salsa is a flavorful workhorse—make like the Casa Ocho team and drizzle it inside tortas, use it as a dip for quesadillas, and add it to chilaquiles.

Salsa Bring 4 cups of water to a boil in a saucepan. Carefully lower in tomatillos, zucchini, and garlic. Cover and cook for 5 minutes, until vegetables are softened.

Meanwhile, heat oil in a skillet over medium heat. Using tongs, add the jalapeño and serrano, cut side down, and fry for 2 minutes. Turn over and fry for another 2 minutes. Remove skillet from heat.

Transfer peppers and oil to a metal bowl. Set aside for 2 minutes to cool.

Using a slotted spoon, add the tomatillos, zucchini, and garlic to the bowl, reserving the cooking water, and let cool. Ladle ½ cup of the reserved cooking water into the bowl and set aside to cool for 5 minutes.

Transfer vegetables and peppers to a blender. Pour in the liquid from the bowl. Add cilantro. Season to taste with salt. Cover blender and blend on high speed for 2 minutes, until thick and smooth. Add a little more reserved cooking water if the salsa verde is too thick. Refrigerate until chilled.

Leftover salsa verde can be stored in an airtight container in the refrigerator for up to 2 weeks.

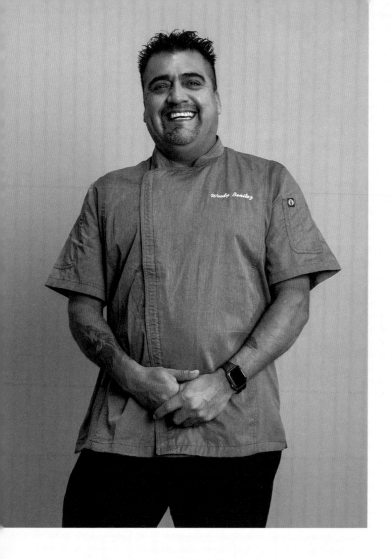

DAVANTI ENOTECA

▶ *LITTLE ITALY* ◀

CHEF / Woody Benitez

IF YOU'VE DINED AT Davanti Enoteca's Little Italy location in the last decade, you may have enjoyed chef Woody Benitez's traditional Italian favorites, such as cacio e pepe (page 43). "Everybody makes it differently," Benitez says. "You need to keep it simple and let the ingredients speak for themselves." His version sticks to the basics: cheese, pepper, and fresh pasta.

Benitez started in Chicago as a dishwasher in the kitchens of Scott Harris Hospitality before earning a place on the line. He then moved to San Diego in 2011 to open Davanti Enoteca's southern California location as its chef.

San Diego's Davanti sits in the heart of Little Italy's thriving dining and nightlife scene. Diners-in-the-know book a table on its private back patio and never skip a chance to start their meals with the Ligurian-style focaccia, served thin with a layer of soft cow's milk cheese and a knob of honeycomb. Those seeking a livelier experience, perhaps during its daily happy hour, hold court in the dining room, at its remodeled twenty-two-seat bar, or al fresco on the front patio. And keeping with its bayside locale and access to local produce, Davanti's menu includes seafood entrées from branzino (page 44) to octopus, and seasonal share plates like corn salad with feta and basil vinaigrette.

It's taken Benitez some time to get used to San Diego's undeniably relaxed pace, but he sees it as an opportunity to experiment in the kitchen. For Benitez, who travels to Italy regularly to learn new techniques to bring back to Davanti Enoteca, food is play, passion, and service. "I love to see people come in and leaving with a smile," he says.

16 oz spaghetti

2 Tbsp extra-virgin olive oil

Pepper

1½ Tbsp butter

2½ Tbsp grated Parmesan

2 Tbsp grated Pecorino-Romano, plus extra for sprinkling

Cacio e Pepe

Sometimes, less is more. Chef Woody Benitez keeps ingredients to a minimum in this recipe but ensures that each and every one are of the best quality to deliver optimal flavor. Benitez recommends using Parmesan and Pecorino-Romano from specialty cheese purveyors Cucina Andolina, if possible.

Pasta Bring a large saucepan of salted water to a boil. Add spaghetti and cook according to package instructions. Drain, reserving 1¼ cups pasta water.

Heat oil in a large skillet over medium heat. Add 17 turns of pepper. Add ¾ cup pasta water, butter, and both cheeses. Slowly stir for 3 to 5 minutes, until creamy. Add the cooked spaghetti to the pan and cook for another 45 to 60 seconds. Remove pan from heat. Adjust the consistency by adding more pasta water, if needed.

Transfer to a large serving platter or individual plates. Finish with a sprinkling of Pecorino-Romano and more pepper.

SHAVED GARLIC IN OIL

2 cups canola oil

20 cloves garlic, thinly sliced

SEA BASS

3 (6-oz) sea bass fillets,
or any white fish fillets

¼ cup canola oil

Salt and pepper, to taste

1 Tbsp Shaved Garlic in Oil (see here)

¼ cup thinly sliced shallots

2 cups whole red and yellow
cherry tomatoes

1 Tbsp jarred crushed Calabrian chilis

¼ cup oregano leaves

3 Tbsp finely chopped parsley

2 Tbsp finely chopped chives

6 Tbsp white wine

¼ cup (½ stick) butter

6 Tbsp vegetable or chicken stock

2 Tbsp fish sauce

Juice of 2 lemons

Crusty bread, to serve

Mediterranean Sea Bass
(*Branzino al Salmoriglio*)

SERVES
3

Mediterranean sea bass is served with salmoriglio sauce, a traditional condiment from Italy's southern region featuring parsley, oregano, and lemon juice.

Shaved garlic in oil Combine the oil and garlic in a bowl or jar and let infuse for at least a day. Refrigerate for up to 7 days.

Sea bass Drizzle sea bass fillets with oil, then sprinkle with salt and pepper. Set aside.

Heat the shaved garlic in oil in a sauté pan over medium heat. Add shallots and sauté for 5 minutes, until translucent. Add tomatoes, chilis, all but 1 teaspoon each of the herbs, and a pinch of salt and cook for another 5 minutes. Deglaze the pan with wine. Add butter, stock, fish sauce, and lemon juice. Remove sauce from heat.

In a separate pan, pan-sear seasoned sea bass fillets over high heat for 3 to 4 minutes on each side.

Assembly Place a fillet in the center of each plate. Spoon sauce on top, then sprinkle with remaining herbs. Season to taste with salt and pepper. Serve with crusty bread.

DOCKSIDE 1953

▶ *MISSION BEACH* ◀

CHEF / Bryan Stuppy

BRYAN STUPPY'S arrival as executive chef of Bahia Resort Hotel's Dockside 1953 ushered in a renewed focus on seafood from local fishmongers. Think oysters and crudos that highlight sea treats like scallops, arctic char, hamachi (Japanese amberjack), and shrimp. Stuppy recalls his initial thought before he even set foot in the building: "Look at this view—we're just steps away from the water and the marina." Guests beeline to Dockside's roomy outdoor patio with its generous view of Mission Bay and the boats. Firepits keep the outdoor vibe going into the evening.

Growing up in Cleveland, Stuppy rarely ate seafood. In its place was an abundance of meat and potatoes (three or four times a week) and hearty Southern dishes made by his Louisville-based grandma. When college and digital media arts didn't capture Stuppy's enthusiasm, he enrolled in Pennsylvania Culinary Institute's Le Cordon Bleu Culinary Arts Program and hit his stride. "I had always loved to cook," Stuppy says. "When I saw chef friends cooking, being creative, and having fun, the kitchen environment drew me in."

After more than a decade wielding knives at a five-star, five-diamond hotel in Colorado and at a prominent hotel in La Jolla, Stuppy now collaborates closely with his Dockside 1953 team to curate a balanced menu of reliable favorites, such as the Drugstore Hamburger, and unexpected gems like roasted carrots with pastrami spices and carrot-top labneh. "People love it," Stuppy says.

SPICY REMOULADE

1¾ cups mayonnaise

2 Tbsp capers, chopped

2 Tbsp chopped cornichons

½ Tbsp finely chopped chives

½ Tbsp finely chopped cilantro

2 Tbsp Dijon mustard

2 anchovy fillets, chopped

½ Tbsp Cajun seasoning

3 dashes Tabasco sauce

3 dashes Worcestershire sauce

Pinch of salt

CRAB CAKES

1¾ tsp Madeira

2 Tbsp stone-ground mustard

¼ cup panko breadcrumbs

2½ Tbsp mayonnaise

Tabasco sauce, to taste

1 large egg, beaten

Salt and white pepper, to taste

1 cup backfin crab meat

1 cup jumbo lump crab meat

1 Tbsp vegetable oil, for frying

Crab Cakes with Spicy Remoulade

SERVES
2–4

Spicy remoulade   Combine all ingredients in a bowl and mix well. Leftover remoulade will keep in an airtight container in the fridge for 7 days.

Crab cakes   Combine all ingredients, except crab meat and oil, in a bowl and mix well. Gently fold in crab meat, taking care not to break it up too much. Form into 4-ounce patties.

Heat oil in a large skillet over medium-high heat. Carefully add crab cakes, spacing them at least ¾ inch apart. Pan-fry for 3 to 5 minutes, until golden brown. Flip and fry for another 3 to 5 minutes, until the internal temperature reaches 145°F. Serve hot with spicy remoulade.

SEARED TUNA

1 Tbsp vegetable oil, for frying

6 oz sushi-grade ahi tuna

Chili-lime seasoning, for coating

PICO DE GALLO

2 Roma tomatoes, seeded and finely chopped

½ small red onion, finely chopped

½ jalapeño, finely chopped

½ bunch cilantro, chopped

1 Tbsp olive oil

Salt and pepper, to taste

GUACAMOLE

2 avocados, peeled and pitted

½ cup Pico de Gallo (see here)

Juice of 2 limes

½ bunch cilantro, chopped

Salt and pepper, to taste

CHIPOTLE CREMA

1 cup Mexican crema (see Note)

½ chipotle pepper in adobo sauce, finely chopped

2 tsp adobo sauce (from chipotle pepper can)

ASSEMBLY

2 Tbsp vegetable oil, for frying

2 (6-inch) corn tortillas

3 Tbsp Guacamole (see here)

2 Tbsp Chipotle Crema (see here), for drizzling

2 radishes, thinly sliced, for garnish

1 jalapeño, thinly sliced, for garnish

3 Tbsp Pico de Gallo (see here), for garnish

Micro cilantro, for garnish

Edible flowers, for garnish (optional)

4 lime wedges, to serve

Ahi Tuna Tostada

Seared tuna Heat oil in a skillet over high heat. Evenly coat tuna with chili-lime seasoning, then add to the pan and sear for 30 seconds on each side. Transfer to a cutting board to let rest and cool. Slice into ¼-inch pieces. Set aside.

Pico de gallo Combine all ingredients and mix well.

Guacamole Place avocados in a bowl, then use a fork to smash. Gently fold in remaining ingredients.

Chipotle crema Combine all ingredients and mix well.

Assembly Heat oil in a clean pan. Fry tortillas for 3 to 4 minutes, until crispy. Transfer tostadas to a paper towel–lined plate to drain. Evenly spread guacamole on each tostada. Top it with tuna and dollops of chipotle crema.

Garnish with radishes, jalapeño, pico de gallo, cilantro, and edible flowers (if using). Serve each tostada with 2 lime wedges.

NOTE Mexican crema can be substituted with plain yogurt or sour cream. Simply dilute with milk or water for a pourable consistency—it should be easy to drizzle over the food.

EXTRAORDINARY DESSERTS

▶ *BANKERS HILL, LITTLE ITALY* ◀

BAKER / Karen Krasne

NATIVE SAN DIEGAN Karen Krasne credits sensual locales like the Hawaiian Islands and Paris as muses for her luscious and covetable confections. Since 1989, Krasne's elaborate cakes, such as the guava and white chocolate mousse layered Shangri-La cake and the Toasted Macadamia Caramel Cheesecake with shortbread crust, have amassed a dedicated following.

What began as an eight-seat café that served only cakes and espresso drinks like lattes and cappuccinos has evolved into a 7,000-square-foot full-service restaurant and patisserie in Little Italy and a Bankers Hill location, where its grilled cheese and Caesar salad with house-made croutons are just as popular as its desserts. In both, an expansive glass case brims with more than thirty types of desserts embellished with edible gold and fresh flowers. The bakery's mousses, cookies, pastries, and ice creams feature over fifteen varieties of Valrhona chocolate alone.

As a college student at the University of Hawaii, Krasne pursued a nutrition degree and worked part-time at a boulangerie. Craving more artistic satisfaction, Krasne moved to Paris to study baking at Le Cordon Bleu. She eventually moved back to San Diego and began baking cakes out of her father's kitchen for Neiman Marcus, special events, and local weddings.

She continues to traverse the globe to push Extraordinary Desserts in new directions. Whether she's reducing the amount of sugar or nixing gelatin in some recipes, or experimenting with Japanese yuzu and matcha or Swedish red currants in others, there are always new techniques to learn and ingredients to discover. "Nothing is forever," Krasne says. But her cakes, like the Gianduia (chocolate mousse, hazelnut buttercream, and boysenberries), her favorite, might be the exception.

▶ *Lemon Meringue Cake*

RICOTTA POUND CAKES

Butter, for greasing

8 large eggs

3 cups sugar

1½ cups grapeseed or vegetable oil

1½ cups ricotta

4 tsp fresh orange juice, strained

1 tsp vanilla extract

4 cups all-purpose flour

4 tsp baking powder

LEMON CURD

2 cups sugar

1 cup fresh lemon juice, strained

8 large eggs

Grated zest of 1 lemon

1 cup (2 sticks) butter, room temperature, cut into ¼-inch cubes

Lemon Meringue Cake

MAKES
1 (10-inch)
cake

"Moist layers of ricotta pound cake surrounded by tart lemon curd and topped with swirls of candy-like meringue create the appeal of both cake and a pie. My favorite way to serve this cake is with fresh summer berries and a berry sauce."

Note that the meringue should only be made once you are ready to decorate the cake.

Ricotta pound cakes Preheat oven to 300°F. Grease two (10- × 3-inch) round cake pans with removable bottoms. Line the bottoms with parchment paper.

In the bowl of a stand mixer fitted with the whisk attachment (or using a hand mixer), combine eggs and sugar and whisk at medium-high speed for 7 minutes, until the mixture falls in heavy ribbons.

In a separate bowl, combine oil, ricotta, orange juice, and vanilla. Gently add the ricotta mixture to the egg mixture and whip until blended.

Sift flour and baking powder into the batter and mix until just incorporated, scraping down the sides of the bowl as needed. Do not overmix. If necessary, use a rubber spatula to fold in the sifted ingredients.

Divide the batter between the cake pans. Place on a rack in the center of the oven and bake for 60 to 75 minutes, until a knife inserted into the centers comes out clean and the tops of the cakes spring back lightly when touched. Set aside to cool.

Remove cakes from the pans and peel the parchment paper from the bottom of each cake. Wrap cakes tightly in plastic wrap until ready to serve.

Cakes can be stored at room temperature for up to a day or in the freezer for a week.

Lemon curd Combine all ingredients except butter in a heatproof, nonreactive bowl. Place over a pan of simmering water (do not allow the bowl to touch the water) and whisk for 4 minutes, until the mixture is frothy and thickens to a custard. (Alternatively, cook until the temperature reaches 190°F on a candy thermometer.) Carefully move the bowl to the counter, then whisk in butter until homogenous and smooth. Strain into a clean, nonreactive

LEMON SIMPLE SYRUP
½ cup sugar
1 cup fresh lemon juice, strained

SWISS MERINGUE
10 egg whites
2½ cups sugar
1 tsp lemon juice

FOR GARNISH
Lemon slices
Edible flower petals (optional)
Edible gold leaf flakes

bowl. Cover with plastic wrap pressed directly onto the surface of the curd. Refrigerate until needed.

The lemon curd can be made up to 3 days in advance and stored in the refrigerator.

Lemon simple syrup   Combine sugar and ¼ cup of water in a small saucepan and bring to a boil over medium-high heat, stirring occasionally. Remove from heat, then pour into a clean bowl and set aside to cool. Stir in lemon juice, until just combined.

Syrup will keep for up to a day in an airtight container in the refrigerator.

Assembly   Place a 10-inch cardboard base in the bottom of a 10- × 3-inch round cake pan with a removable bottom. Using a serrated knife, slice the tops off each cake so that each cake is even. Slice each cake horizontally into two even layers.

Place a cake disk into the prepared pan. Moisten surface with lemon simple syrup, then spread 1⅓ cups of lemon curd on top. Repeat with three more layers of cake, ending with the lemon curd. Wrap the cake with its pan in plastic wrap and freeze for a minimum of 24 hours.

Two to four hours before serving, remove the assembled cake from freezer.

Swiss meringue   Prepare the Swiss meringue within two to four hours before serving. In a medium heatproof bowl, combine egg whites, sugar, and lemon juice. Set over a pan of simmering water (do not allow the bowl to touch the water) and whisk continuously for 4 minutes, until hot and frothy. (Alternatively, cook until the temperature reaches 170°F on a candy thermometer.)

Transfer the mixture to the bowl of a stand mixer fitted with the whisk attachment (or use a hand mixer). Whip on high speed for 6 minutes, until cooled, glossy, and tripled in volume.

Assembly   Unwrap cake and transfer to a cutting board. Using a spatula, spread the Swiss meringue generously over the top and sides, creating swirl-like peaks. Using a propane torch, lightly burn the edges of the meringue until browned.

Decorate with lemon slices, flower petals (if using), and edible gold leaf flakes. Refrigerate until ready to serve.

1⅔ cups Bob's Red Mill Gluten Free 1-to-1 Baking Flour

¾ tsp baking soda

¾ tsp fleur de sel

1½ tsp Ener-G Egg Replacer

2⅓ cups packed brown sugar

½ cup Miyoko's Plant Milk Butter, room temperature

3 Tbsp almond milk

1 Tbsp vanilla extract

¾ cup smooth peanut butter

½ cup roasted, unsalted peanuts, chopped, plus extra for sprinkling

½ cup unsweetened shredded coconut

Aloha Peanut Butter Cookies

"This recipe was inspired by a jar of coconut-flavored peanut butter I purchased in Oahu. Peanut butter and coconut pack a lot of moisture, so this gluten-free vegan cookie still has the soft chewiness I love in a peanut butter cookie."

To mix things up, replace the peanut butter with your favorite nut butter and add chunks of dark chocolate. You could also dip the cookies in melted dark chocolate.

Cookies In a large bowl, sift together flour, baking soda, and fleur de sel.

Put 2 teaspoons of water in a small bowl. Sprinkle egg replacer on top to dissolve.

In the bowl of a stand mixer fitted with the paddle attachment, combine the brown sugar and vegan butter and mix until creamy. Add the egg replacer mixture and mix until just incorporated. Stir in almond milk and vanilla, taking care not to overmix.

Scrape down the sides of the bowl, then add peanut butter and mix until just blended. (Again, do not overmix; otherwise, the mixture will turn greasy.)

Add the flour mixture and mix carefully. Stir in peanuts and coconut. Cover dough with plastic wrap and refrigerate overnight.

Preheat oven to 325°F.

Using a ⅓-cup scoop or measuring cup, measure out 12 cookies. Place the cookies on a baking sheet, slightly flattened into disks and evenly spaced 2 inches apart. Sprinkle chopped peanuts on top. Bake for 20 minutes, until golden brown—they will be crispy on the outside and chewy in the center.

GLASS BOX

▶ *DEL MAR* ◀

CHEF / Ethan Yang

THE FIRST thing one notices about Ethan Yang's restaurant is its gleaming sushi bar, enclosed in glass. "What you see is what you get," says Yang, executive chef of Glass Box in Del Mar Heights. And what guests get is beautifully prepared nigiri and sushi rolls featuring locally caught and Japan-sourced fish accented with plays on traditional sauces and condiments like dragon fruit ponzu and togarashi salt.

Before opening Glass Box, Yang spent his formative years assisting in his dad's restaurant—from boiling chicken to filleting fish. He honed his fine-dining skills at Carvers Steaks & Chops in Rancho Bernardo and Pechanga Resort Casino. Though Glass Box's sushi bar is a focal point, the restaurant accommodates tables for families or larger parties and also offers a range of Asian-inspired cocktails, like its Wagyu-washed old fashioned. It's common to find seasonal specials crafted from collaborations between Yang and his team—their version of duck confit salad sees five-spice-and-soy-marinated duck, goat cheese, and stone fruit tossed in ume-champagne vinaigrette.

Larger dishes like Taiwanese beef noodle soup (page 60) also hit the mark. When Glass Box opened as part of the Sky Deck in 2022, the hours-long-simmered beef shank and hand-pulled noodles swimming in a savory five-spice-perfumed broth became a quick favorite. "I never thought the dish would take off the way it did," Yang says.

HAMACHI

1 tsp Sichuan peppercorns

1 tsp coriander seeds

1 tsp red chili flakes

¼ cup mirin

¼ cup dry sake

3 Tbsp salt

3 Tbsp cane sugar

2 cups ponzu

2 sheets kombu

1 (9-oz) sushi-grade, skinless hamachi (Japanese amberjack) fillet

PICKLED TOMATOES AND ONION

6 heirloom cherry tomatoes

1 red onion, thinly sliced

Cured Hamachi with Edamame-Avocado Purée

SERVES
4–6

This hamachi (Japanese amberjack) dish was inspired by chef Ethan Yang's travels to Miyazaki, Japan, where he cooked alongside local chefs and visited artisans who were producing the best ingredients. "We created this edamame purée one evening when we were experimenting with excess edamame," Yang says. "I took that idea back to the States and created this recipe."

Hamachi In a skillet, combine peppercorns, coriander seeds, and chili flakes and toast over medium heat, until fragrant. Take care not to burn the spices. Add mirin and sake and boil until the alcohol cooks off. Pour into a small mixing bowl. Stir in salt, sugar, and ponzu. Strain the curing liquid, then set aside to cool.

Soak kombu in a bowl of water and set aside until softened.

Place hamachi in a shallow container. Pour in enough curing liquid to coat the fish. (Reserve the rest to pickle onion and tomatoes.) Marinate for 5 minutes on each side.

Remove hamachi from liquid and transfer to a cutting board. Wrap it with the kombu, then wrap in plastic wrap and refrigerate for 2 to 3 hours to cure. This will infuse the kombu flavor and firm up the texture of the fish.

Pickled tomatoes and onion In a bowl, combine tomatoes, onion, and the remaining pickling liquid. Set aside for 15 to 20 minutes.

EDAMAME-AVOCADO PURÉE

½ cup shelled edamame

2 avocados, pitted, peeled, and diced

1 jalapeño, thinly sliced

¼ cup olive oil

½ tsp salt

½ tsp sugar

¼ tsp granulated garlic

Bunch of cilantro leaves

Pea shoots or pea microgreens, for garnish

Edamame-avocado purée Meanwhile, bring a large saucepan of salted water to a rolling boil. Prepare an ice bath in a large bowl. Lower edamame into the pan and blanch for 30 seconds. Using a slotted spoon, transfer them into the ice bath. Drain.

Transfer edamame to a food processor, reserving 2 tablespoons for garnish. Add the remaining ingredients except the pea shoots and process on high speed for a minute, until smooth.

The purée can be stored in an airtight container in the refrigerator for a day.

Assembly Remove hamachi from the refrigerator and wipe off the excess cure. Cut into ¼-inch-thick slices, either straight down or with your knife at a slight angle of no more than 15 degrees.

Place a dollop of edamame purée slightly off center on each plate. Shingle 4 hamachi slices across the edamame purée. Garnish with pickled tomatoes and onion, reserved edamame beans, and pea shoots (or microgreens).

Serve immediately.

10 beef marrow bones

2 Tbsp canola oil

1 Tbsp sliced ginger

6 cloves garlic

1 white onion, thinly sliced

10 scallions, chopped with roots and whites separated from greens

8 Chinese dates (see Note)

5 dried Japanese chili peppers (see Note)

8 pods cardamom

6 star anise

2 bay leaves

1 small cinnamon stick

2 Tbsp black peppercorns

1 Tbsp cloves

1 Tbsp fennel seeds

3 lbs boneless beef shank, cut into 1-inch cubes

¼ cup Shaoxing cooking wine

3½ Tbsp fermented bean paste (*doubanjiang*)

¼ cup soy sauce

¼ cup mushroom-flavored dark soy sauce

3 Tbsp oyster sauce

2 Tbsp sugar

¾ tsp salt

1 Tbsp chicken bouillon powder

8 baby bok choy

1 (14-oz) package Chinese wheat noodles

Cilantro, for garnish

Chili crisp, for garnish

Taiwanese Beef Noodle Soup

SERVES 4

While Taiwanese beef noodle soup is a family favorite in the Yang household, and ubiquitous in the island of Taiwan, it's trickier to find in San Diego. Yang and his father, a chef himself, have been experimenting with the dish for years but developed the Glass Box recipe over six months—identifying the ideal cut of beef and perfecting the flavorful broth.

Soup Combine marrow bones and 8 cups of water in a large stockpot. Bring to a boil, then cover and reduce to medium-low heat. Simmer for at least 8 hours, until it's reduced by a quarter. The longer it simmers, the richer the flavor. Strain stock, then set aside to cool. Beef stock can be made ahead and stored in the refrigerator for up to 4 days.

Heat oil in a wok over medium-high heat until hot. Add ginger and garlic and sauté for 2 minutes, until dark golden brown. Add onion and scallion roots and whites (reserving the greens for later) and sauté for another 2 minutes, until light brown.

Add Chinese dates, Japanese chilis, and spices. Fry for 1 minute, until fragrant and slightly toasted. Add beef shank and brown for 2 to 3 minutes. Stir in cooking wine.

In a bowl, combine fermented bean paste, both soy sauces, oyster sauce, and sugar. Whisk for 1 to 2 minutes, until well combined. Add to the wok.

Transfer the mixture to a stockpot. Pour in the prepared beef stock, cover, and boil over high heat for 45 minutes. Add salt and chicken bouillon. Reduce heat to low, cover, and simmer for another 2 hours. Strain stock, reserving beef. Keep warm.

Bring a small saucepan of water to a boil. Add bok choy and cook for 2 to 3 minutes.

Cook wheat noodles according to package instructions.

To serve, divide the cooked noodles among the serving bowls. Add bok choy and beef. Ladle stock on top, then garnish with the reserved scallion greens, cilantro, and chili crisp.

NOTE Chinese dates (also known as jujubes or red dates) and dried Japanese chili peppers—which are actually native to Mexico—can be purchased at Asian markets, specialty grocers, or online.

JRDN

▶ *PACIFIC BEACH* ◀

CHEF / Jerry Ranson

WITH AN INVITING outdoor patio space, an enviable location just steps from the ocean, and a menu touting longtime hits like steamed mussels in a creamy tomato broth and a lobster BLT sandwich, JRDN at Tower23 Hotel embodies the coastal lifestyle from every angle. The restaurant, located in Pacific Beach, is a versatile place for special occasion surf and turf dinners and more casual post-beach meals.

The restaurant's famous mussels dish has been an original menu item and a guest favorite since its opening nineteen years ago, and it's not going anywhere. "I pride myself on being consistent," says executive chef Jerry Ranson, who assumed the role in 2023. Before JRDN, Ranson oversaw culinary operations at nearby Belmont Park.

Understandably, JRDN's seaside locale means many of JRDN's guests come for the seafood, like its whole fried snapper, scallops, and sushi rolls. Additionally, JRDN serves salads, pastas, and steaks with a selection of sauces, including bone marrow demi salsa verde, chimichurri, and ancho chile béarnaise.

In the kitchen, Ranson leans on his tenure in the Navy, where he began his culinary career, to harmoniously lead his team. During that time, Ranson learned to read recipes, lead a kitchen team, and navigate an environment where there's always something to do—in a compressed window of time, and at a standard that demands quality among the chaos. "The Navy put me in a position to lead," Ranson says.

- 2 lbs fresh black mussels
- 1 cup diced Spanish chorizo
- 4 cloves garlic, chopped (2 Tbsp)
- 2 Tbsp chopped shallots
- 1 cup white wine
- 1 cup chunky tomato sauce
- 1 cup heavy cream
- 2 Tbsp butter
- 2 Tbsp chopped parsley, chives, and/or tarragon
- 1 tsp red chili flakes
- Juice of 1 lemon
- Salt and pepper, to taste
- Pea tendrils or other fresh herbs, for garnish
- 1 French baguette, sliced and grilled, to serve

JRDN's Steamed Mussels

Fresh mussels and chorizo are the stars of this creamy, brothy, tomato-based dish that's finished with a bit of chili heat. Serve with grilled bread to sop up the extra broth.

Mussels Wash mussels in cold water, removing any stringy beards. Discard any mussels that don't close when tapped.

Heat a large skillet over medium heat. Add chorizo and cook for 1 to 2 minutes, until fat is rendered. Don't burn the chorizo—this first step sets the flavor for the entire dish. Add mussels, garlic, and shallots and sauté for another minute. Add wine and simmer until reduced by half.

Pour in tomato sauce and cream and stir to incorporate. Cover and steam for another 3 minutes, until mussels open. Uncover, then stir in butter, herbs, chili flakes, and lemon juice. Once butter has melted, season with salt and pepper. Discard any mussels that don't open.

Pour into your favorite serving bowl. Garnish with pea tendrils (or other fresh herbs) and serve with grilled bread.

CILANTRO PESTO

2 cloves garlic

¼ cup grated Parmesan

Bunch of cilantro, leaves only

Juice of 1 lemon

Salt and pepper, to taste

¼ cup olive oil

SMOKED HONEY BABA GHANOUSH

1 eggplant

¼ cup olive oil, plus extra for brushing

Salt and pepper, to taste

2 cloves garlic

1 Tbsp tahini

1 Tbsp honey

¼ tsp ground cumin

¼ tsp ground coriander

Juice of 1 lemon

DUKKAH

2 Tbsp sesame seeds

2 Tbsp ground coriander

1 Tbsp pepitas (pumpkin seeds)

1 Tbsp hazelnuts

1 tsp ground cumin

Salt and pepper, to taste

Lamb Lollipops with Cilantro Pesto, Smoked Honey Baba Ghanoush, and Dukkah

SERVES
4—6

These lamb lollipops are designed for sharing. Paired with a vibrant cilantro pesto and a smoky baba ghanoush for a playful appetizer, they are perfect for gatherings or special occasions.

Cilantro pesto Combine all ingredients except oil in a blender. Blend for 10 seconds, then turn off and stir ingredients with a wooden spoon. Blend again and repeat four times.

With the motor running on low speed, slowly drizzle in oil. Adjust seasoning to taste.

Smoked honey baba ghanoush Prepare a smoker or charcoal grill. (Alternatively, preheat oven to 400°F to bake eggplant. You just won't get that smoky flavor.)

Peel eggplant to remove outer skin, then trim off top and bottom ends. Slice eggplant into 1-inch rounds. Brush each side with oil, then season with salt and pepper.

Place on the grill and grill each side for 4 minutes, until eggplant is slightly charred and soft. (Or bake for 18 to 20 minutes.) Transfer eggplant to a plate and set aside to cool.

In a blender, combine eggplant and the remaining ingredients except oil. Blend for 10 seconds, then turn off and stir ingredients with a wooden spoon. Blend again and repeat four times.

With the motor running on low speed, slowly drizzle in oil. Season with salt and pepper.

Dukkah Preheat oven to 325°F.

Evenly spread all ingredients, except salt and pepper, on a baking sheet. Toast seeds, nuts, and spices for 5 to 7 minutes, until fragrant and the edges of the hazelnuts turn slightly golden brown. Remove from oven and season to taste with salt and pepper. Set aside to cool. Place in a spice or coffee grinder and pulse until coarsely ground.

LAMB LOLLIPOPS
2 (22- to 24-oz) lamb racks
2 Tbsp olive oil
Salt and pepper, to taste

Lamb lollipops Preheat a grill over high heat.

Using a knife, cut lamb between the bones into 8 lollipops per rack. Lightly oil lamb and season both sides with salt and pepper. Add lamb to the grill and grill for 3 minutes. Do a quarter turn and cook for another minute. Flip each lamb lollipop and grill for another 2 minutes. Do a quarter turn and cook for another minute. Transfer lamb to a cutting board and set aside to rest for 5 minutes.

Assembly With a spatula, spread baba ghanoush across a serving plate, about ½ inch thick. Fan out lamb lollipops across the plate. Spoon cilantro pesto on top. Finish with a generous sprinkling of dukkah.

KETTNER EXCHANGE

▶ *LITTLE ITALY* ◀

CHEF / Brian Redzikowski

WHEN KETTNER EXCHANGE (KEX) opened in Little Italy in 2014, the historic area was nowhere near the bustling restaurant destination it is today. At that time, Brian Redzikowski contemplated moving back to New York, or maybe to San Francisco. "It was a sleepy surf town when I arrived here twelve years ago," he says. He stayed to open Kettner Exchange and witnessed both restaurant and neighborhood become and remain as lively as ever. On a Friday night, KEX serves 2,000 plates between its two floors, which also includes an open-air cocktail bar and lounge on the top floor.

As corporate executive chef of SDCM Restaurant Group, Redzikowski oversees a menu rooted in French cooking techniques and Asian influences and informed by local and regional farms offering seasonal ingredients like spring ramps and summer tomatoes. There are hints of playfulness throughout KEX's menu, too. The duck meatball is a cheeky nod to its Little Italy locale. The kale salad has been a mainstay since opening night. With raisins, toasted almonds, Parmesan, and a lemon vinaigrette, "it's sweet, sour, and has all kinds of goodies in it," Redzikowski says.

Redzikowski spent much of his youth in upstate New York, where he tended to his family's garden and raised and butchered chickens. His tenure as chef includes three-Michelin-starred Joël Robuchon in Las Vegas and Matsuhisa in Aspen. Since choosing to stay in San Diego, Redzikowski has opened more restaurants as part of SDCM, including The Grass Skirt in Pacific Beach and The Waverly in Cardiff.

LEMON-PEPPER DRESSING

2 lemons

2 ice cubes

3 Tbsp sugar

¼ tsp pepper

Pinch of salt

½ cup grapeseed oil

KALE SALAD

4 cups thinly sliced purple and green kale

¼ cup grated Parmesan

¼ cup golden raisins

¼ cup sliced almonds, toasted

1 small apple, thinly sliced (optional)

Salt and pepper, to taste

Kale Salad with Lemon-Pepper Dressing

SERVES
4

"This salad was inspired by a conversation I had with my older brother, who owns three restaurants in Colorado. He had a kale salad on his menu, which had become a staple, and I always thought a kale salad was boring and uninspiring. Though I have yet to try my brother's salad, I came up with this variation as we opened Kettner Exchange and it has become the most requested recipe by our guests."

Lemon-pepper dressing Carefully segment lemons, then squeeze as much lemon juice from the remaining core into a blender. Add the segments and remaining ingredients and blend on high speed for 2 minutes. Strain.

Kale salad Combine all ingredients in a large bowl. Add ¼ cup lemon-pepper dressing and toss to mix. Serve immediately.

CHERMOULA

4 cloves garlic

Bunch of cilantro

2 Tbsp paprika

1 Tbsp ground cumin

1 tsp salt

1 tsp grated ginger

½ tsp cayenne pepper

3 Tbsp canola oil

2 Tbsp lemon juice

BULGUR

1 cup bulgur

Pinch of salt

1 Tbsp olive oil

TOMATO

1 Roma tomato, scored

1 clove garlic, smashed

1 sprig thyme

Salt and pepper, to taste

2 tsp extra-virgin olive oil

EGGPLANT

2 to 3 Tbsp canola oil, for frying

4 Chinese eggplants, sliced into 1-inch disks

Salt, to taste

½ cup Chermoula (see here)

CRISPY KATAIFI

2 to 3 Tbsp canola oil, for frying

1 cup shredded kataifi, loosely packed

TOASTED PINE NUTS

1 tsp butter

1 Tbsp + 1 tsp pine nuts

ASSEMBLY

½ cup plain yogurt

16 mint leaves

16 cilantro leaves

16 Italian parsley leaves

1 Tbsp lemon juice

1 Tbsp extra-virgin olive oil

Roasted Chinese Eggplant with Bulgur and Chermoula

SERVES 4

"At our restaurants, we use this very versatile chermoula on fish, meats, and vegetables."

Chermoula Combine all ingredients in a blender and blend until smooth. Refrigerate until needed.

Bulgur Combine all ingredients in a small saucepan. Add ½ cup of water, then bring to a simmer and cover. Cook for 12 minutes, until bulgur is fully cooked and dry. Remove from heat and fluff with a fork. Set aside at room temperature.

Tomato Preheat oven to 250°F and line a baking sheet with parchment paper. Prepare a small bowl of ice water. Bring a pot of water to a boil. Blanch tomato for 12 seconds, then immediately remove and shock in cold water. Peel tomato, then cut into quarters and remove seeds. On the prepared baking sheet, toss tomato pieces with garlic, thyme, salt, pepper, and oil. Bake for 2½ hours. Set aside.

Eggplant Preheat oven to 350°F.

Heat oil in a large skillet over medium-high heat. Season eggplant disks with salt, then add to pan and sear for 3 minutes per side, until golden brown and soft. Work in batches if needed.

Transfer to a baking sheet and top with chermoula. Bake for 5 to 7 minutes, until golden brown.

Crispy kataifi Heat oil in a pan on medium-high heat, then add kataifi and fry until golden brown, about 30 seconds. Set aside.

Toasted pine nuts Melt butter in a small pan on low heat. Add pine nuts and toast until golden brown, about 4 minutes. Drain and set aside.

Assembly Add yogurt to a plate and smear in a circle. Add the bulgur, then place the eggplant on top.

Place tomatoes on top of the eggplant. Top with kataifi and pine nuts, sprinkle with herbs, and finish with lemon juice and a drizzle of oil.

LA CLOCHETTE

▶ *PACIFIC BEACH* ◀

CHEF / Blake Chisholm

OUTSIDE, UMBRELLAS fan out over the bistro tables that pepper the sidewalk, offering a respite from the San Diego sun. Inside, find a glass case stocked with sweet and savory pastries, and an all-day menu with global spins on classic French dishes. Opened in 2020, Pacific Beach's La Clochette is run by sibling founders Willy Wu Jye Hwa and Karine Beers. Originally from Madagascar, they passed on cities like Montreal and Paris and adopted San Diego as home. They partnered with executive chef Blake Chisholm, a Louisiana native who moved to San Diego after he tried surfing during a beach vacation in Texas. "Technically, I didn't even surf. I just felt the force and [knew I couldn't] live without it."

Together, they've created a casual café experience informed by their international perspectives. La Clochette's duck brandy tartine, for example, is rooted in classic French techniques, from sautéing vegetables and aromatics as a sauce base to deglazing with brandy to build flavor to adding cream. Chisholm also revives day-old bread that would otherwise be lost as an homage to a humble European tradition that made its way to the South (page 75). The chef, who grew up in New Orleans, says every generation prepared food this way: "When I was a child, when my parents were kids, and their parents were kids, they took all the old bread, dipped it in eggs, griddled it, and then put a really heavy sauce or stew overtop."

On any given day, one can pop into La Clochette for an artfully crafted latte and an almond croissant or a pastrami-cured tuna sandwich with almond pesto on a toasted, yet pliable, baguette. For Chisholm, La Clochette is the confluence of years of culinary experience. "It's one of those rare instances where your career path culminates and brings you to something where you can apply your skills and education."

8 cups canola oil or peanut oil,
  for frying
½ oz dry active yeast
½ cup sugar
4½ cups flour, plus extra for dusting
¼ cup (½ stick) butter, melted
½ cup milk
1½ tsp salt
Powdered sugar, for dusting
Coffee, to serve

Beignets

Warm, fried, and sugar-dusted beignets remind chef Blake Chisholm of his childhood in Louisiana. These days, he pairs them with coffee—a combination for a great morning.

Beignets Add oil to a large, deep frying pan. Oil should not fill the pan more than halfway. Heat oil over medium heat until a candy or deep-fry thermometer reads 350°F.

In the bowl of a stand mixer fitted with the hook attachment, combine yeast, ½ cup of warm water (no more than 100°F), and sugar and mix for 1 minute. Let stand for 10 minutes. Mixture will become foamy and smell like alcohol.

Add flour, butter, and milk, then the salt. Mix with the dough hook for about 10 minutes. Dough should have a lot of elasticity.

Remove dough from bowl and let rest for 5 minutes. Using a rolling pin, roll dough out on a lightly floured surface into a large rectangle about ¼ inch thick. Cut into 2-inch squares and deep-fry immediately. Turn the frying dough every 30 seconds to ensure each side browns evenly. After about 2 minutes, once the dough is golden brown on all sides, remove from the fryer and immediately dust generously with powdered sugar so the sugar will stick to the beignets. Serve warm with nice strong coffee and enjoy.

Ingredients

LEMONGRASS-BRAISED CHICKEN

1 cup sugar

¼ cup olive oil

4 chicken leg quarters

Salt and pepper, to taste

2 stalks lemongrass

¼ cup garlic cloves

½ cup fish sauce

TARTINE

½ cup (1 stick) unsalted European butter (divided) (see Note)

4 to 6 slices sourdough bread

6 free-range eggs, beaten

4 cloves garlic, chopped

1 large red bell pepper, seeded, deveined, and sliced

1 cup chopped scallions, plus extra for garnish

2 cups Lemongrass-Braised Chicken (see here)

½ cup brandy

2 cups heavy cream

Pepper, to taste

1 lime, quartered

Microgreens, for garnish

NOTE European butter is typically creamier than North American butter due to its higher butterfat content.

Lemongrass Chicken Brandy Tartine

SERVES 4–6

"Growing up in the American South, this dish transformed stale bread, saving it from going to waste," says Blake Chisholm. "It combines Vietnamese and Cajun French influences beautifully, born from a career of blending cultures and techniques. It's delicious and budget conscious."

Lemongrass-braised chicken In a saucepan, combine sugar and 2 cups of water and boil over high heat, until sugar has completely dissolved. Set aside.

Heat oil in a large, high-sided skillet over high heat. Season chicken with salt and pepper. Add to the pan, skin side down, and pan-fry for 3 minutes, until brown. Turn over and fry for another 3 minutes, until brown and caramelized.

Add lemongrass, garlic, fish sauce, and the sugar water. Reduce heat to medium-low and cover. Simmer for 1 hour, or until tender. Flip leg quarters, cover, and cook over low heat for another hour. The sauce should fill the pan halfway for the full braising time. If needed, add more water.

Transfer the chicken to a plate and set aside. Increase heat to high, bring the sauce to a boil, and cook until thickened.

When chicken is cool enough to handle, shred meat. Discard bones.

Strain the sauce and combine with the meat and set aside.

Tartine Melt ¼ cup (½ stick) butter in a large skillet over medium heat. Soak both sides of the bread slices in the egg and add to the pan, working in batches if needed. Fry for 2 minutes on each side, until golden brown. Transfer to a plate and set aside.

In the same skillet, melt the remaining ¼ cup (½ stick) butter over high heat. Add garlic, bell pepper, and scallions and sauté for 2 minutes, until soft and lightly caramelized. Add lemongrass-braised chicken and cook, stirring occasionally, for 5 minutes, until the bottom of the pan browns. Slowly add brandy, watching carefully as the alcohol is cooked off and the flames die down. Stir in cream and season with pepper. Reduce heat to medium and cook for 2 to 3 minutes, until sauce thickens.

Assembly Place a fried bread slice on a plate. Spoon lemongrass chicken sauce on top, then add a squeeze of lime. Garnish with scallions and microgreens and serve immediately.

LILIAN'S

▶ *RANCHO SANTA FE* ◀

CHEF / Moira Hill

MOIRA HILL always enjoyed cooking. Once entrenched in the culinary world, her ambition earned her an executive chef role before she turned thirty. She considered another path, though her grandfather's words offered a compass. "Do something you love, and not something you feel like you have to do," he would tell her.

As executive chef of Lilian's at The Inn at Rancho Santa Fe, Hill brings a passion for whole animal butchery, seasonality, and zero-waste practices to the coastal Californian menu, which includes a crispy-skin Monterey Bay king salmon dish served with artichoke heart purée, lentil salad, and local citrus slaw. "It's difficult, but it inspires me," she says of her commitment to sustainable cooking practices. Lilian's interiors have also gone green, literally, as guests dine in a glamorous space wrapped in emerald latticework.

Chef Hill is no stranger to refined cooking. The San Diego native notes her formative years at George's at the Cove, Juniper and Ivy, and Campfire helped shape her culinary approach. And no matter what kitchen she presides over, she strives to add an element of surprise to every dish, whether it be a spicy kick or perhaps a crunch. The question is always, "What can I do to make a dish a little bit different?"

▶ *Kale Ricotta Cavatelli Pasta with Spiced Lamb Sausage and Arrabbiata Sauce and Roasted Brussels Sprouts with Honey-Chili Glaze and Sesame Dressing*

HONEY-CHILI GLAZE

2 Tbsp vegetable oil

5 bird's eye chilis, chopped

3 cloves garlic

1 yellow onion, chopped

½ cup + 2 Tbsp rice wine vinegar

½ cup + 2 Tbsp soy sauce

1 cup honey

½ cup gochujang paste

Salt, to taste

SESAME DRESSING

½ cup sesame seeds, toasted and ground

½ cup Kewpie mayonnaise

2 Tbsp rice wine vinegar

4 tsp soy sauce

4 tsp sugar

4 tsp sesame oil

Salt, to taste

BRUSSELS SPROUTS

2 lbs Brussels sprouts, trimmed and halved lengthwise

2 Tbsp olive oil

1 Tbsp salt

1 Tbsp sesame oil

½ lb firm tofu, cut into ½-inch cubes

3 to 4 Tbsp Honey-Chili Glaze (see here)

1 cup roasted peanuts, chopped

Bunch of scallions, thinly sliced, for garnish

Roasted Brussels Sprouts with Honey-Chili Glaze and Sesame Dressing

Roasted Brussels get the spicy-sweet treatment with a honey-chili glaze—but it doesn't stop there. A creamy sesame-soy drizzle ups the complexity, while roasted peanuts lend a textural crunch.

Honey-chili glaze Heat oil in a skillet over medium-high heat. Add chilis, garlic, and onion and sauté for 1 to 2 minutes. Add vinegar and soy sauce to deglaze. Stir in honey and gochujang paste. Set aside to cool slightly.

Transfer mixture to a blender and blend until smooth. Season to taste with salt.

Sesame dressing Combine all ingredients in a blender and blend until smooth. Season to taste with salt.

Brussels sprouts Preheat oven to 450°F.

Toss Brussels sprouts in olive oil, add salt, and place on a baking sheet. Roast for 10 to 15 minutes, until tender. Transfer to a skillet. Add sesame oil and sear over high heat for 2 to 3 minutes, until cooked through. Add tofu and cook for another 2 to 3 minutes, until warmed through.

Add honey-chili glaze and toss to coat. Add peanuts and toss again. Transfer to a plate, drizzle with sesame dressing, and garnish with scallions.

LAMB SAUSAGE

1 Tbsp ground cumin

1 Tbsp garlic powder

½ Tbsp ground coriander

½ Tbsp dried parsley

½ Tbsp dried oregano

2 tsp salt

1 tsp paprika

¼ tsp cayenne pepper

2½ lbs ground lamb

KALE PUREE

1 lb black kale, destemmed

1 Tbsp olive oil

1 tsp salt

PASTA DOUGH

2¾ cups "OO" flour, plus extra for dusting

2¼ cups durum flour

1 lb ricotta

3 eggs

¼ cup Kale Puree (see here)

¾ tsp salt

ARRABBIATA SAUCE

1 (14-oz) can Bianco whole peeled tomatoes

½ cup heavy cream

½ Tbsp red chili flakes

Salt, to taste

Kale Ricotta Cavatelli Pasta with Spiced Lamb Sausage and Arrabbiata Sauce

SERVES
4–6

Chef Moira Hill uses a pasta maker with a cavatelli attachment or a wooden cavatelli board to prepare the pasta. Alternatively, you can cut the dough into fettuccine.

Lamb sausage Combine spices in a large bowl. Add lamb and mix well. Cook off a small piece of sausage to test the seasoning. Adjust as needed.

The lamb mixture can be made up to 3 days in advance and refrigerated in an airtight container until needed.

Kale puree Fill a bowl with ice water. Bring a small saucepan of water to a boil. Add kale and blanch for 1 to 2 minutes. Drain pot, then shock kale in the ice bath.

In a blender, combine kale, oil, 1 tablespoon of water, and salt and blend until smooth and slightly thick.

Pasta dough Combine both flours in a bowl and mix well.

In the bowl of a large stand mixer fitted with the hook attachment, combine ricotta, eggs, kale puree, and salt and beat until combined. Add half of the flour and mix. Slowly add the remaining flour and mix until a dough has formed.

Transfer dough to a clean surface lightly dusted with flour. Knead for a minute, then divide dough in half. Wrap each piece in plastic wrap and refrigerate for at least 1 hour.

To make the cavatelli rolls, form cavatelli pasta per manufacturer's instructions, depending on your device. (Alternatively, you can cut the dough into fettuccine.)

Arrabbiata sauce In a saucepan, combine tomatoes, cream, and chili flakes and bring to a simmer over medium heat. Simmer for 15 to 20 minutes, stirring occasionally. Blend with an immersion blender until smooth. Season to taste with salt.

ASSEMBLY

1 Tbsp vegetable oil
1 large yellow onion, finely chopped
6 large cloves garlic, finely chopped
1 Tbsp butter
Salt, to taste
¼ bunch basil, torn, for garnish
Ricotta, for topping

Assembly Heat oil in a large saucepan over medium-high heat. Add onion and garlic and sauté for 7 minutes, until slightly translucent. Increase heat to high, then add the butter and the lamb sausage and sear for 2 to 3 minutes, breaking the sausage up into pieces. Add the sauce, reduce heat to medium, and simmer for 15 minutes.

Bring salted water to a boil in a large saucepan. Add fresh cavatelli and boil for 2 to 3 minutes, until cooked through. Drain, reserving a little pasta water.

Add pasta to sauce. Remove from heat and toss to combine. If needed, thin out with a little pasta water. Season to taste with salt.

Transfer to a serving plate and garnish with torn basil and dollops of ricotta.

LOUISIANA PURCHASE

▶ *NORTH PARK* ◀

CHEF / Quinnton Austin

WHEN QUINNTON AUSTIN moved to San Diego in 2018 to join Grind & Prosper, the hospitality group behind Louisiana Purchase and Q and A Restaurant & Oyster Bar, he brought the vibrant culture of New Orleans with him. At Louisiana Purchase in North Park, Austin showcases the Big Easy's multifaceted flavors and ingredients, from its hit savory alligator and andouille sausage cheesecake with crawfish sauce to fried lemon pepper catfish and Crawfish Monica Rib Eye (page 83). "We do more than jambalaya and étouffée," Austin says of his hometown cuisine.

Austin was in college when Hurricane Katrina displaced a million New Orleans residents in 2005. He gained a campus reputation for what he could make with a hot plate and George Foreman Grill. Students and professors would line up for his dorm-room steaks, fried chicken, and fish. "Anything we could get with the FEMA card," Austin recalls. He eventually went on to culinary school in the area. He's appreciative of that experience, which, as part of the curriculum, taught him to research a dish's provenance. He also juggled several cook positions in-between. It sounds intense, but to Austin, the energy of the kitchen relaxed him. "That was always my thing, my good times, my safe spot."

1½ cups heavy cream

3 cloves garlic, finely chopped

½ sprig rosemary

1 Tbsp Cajun seasoning

Cayenne pepper, to taste

6 oz crawfish tail meat, finely chopped

2 Tbsp grated Parmesan

½ lemon

Salt, to taste

1 (1-lb) rib eye steak

2 Tbsp Cajun seasoning

2 tsp salt

1 clove garlic, chopped

Sprig of rosemary

3 sprigs thyme (divided)

½ cup olive oil, plus extra for frying

2 Tbsp Worcestershire sauce

2 Tbsp A.1. Sauce

½ cup (1 stick) + 2 Tbsp butter

Crawfish Monica Rib Eye

SERVES
2–4

Crawfish Monica is a classic Louisiana dish marrying the succulent crustaceans with a delectable sauce made using cream, garlic, and spices. Here, chef Quinnton Austin pairs the sauce with a juicy rib eye steak.

Crawfish sauce Heat cream in a saucepan over medium heat. Add garlic, rosemary, Cajun seasoning and cayenne pepper and simmer for 5 to 7 minutes, until reduced. Stir in crawfish and Parmesan, then squeeze in lemon juice. Season to taste with salt. Sauce should be creamy and slightly spicy.

Steak Pierce steak all over with a fork. Rub in Cajun seasoning and salt on both sides. In a bowl, combine garlic, rosemary, and 1 thyme sprig. Add oil, Worcestershire sauce, and A.1. Sauce and mix well. Pour over steak, then refrigerate for 1 hour.

Set steak aside for 15 minutes at room temperature to warm up.

Pour in enough oil to cover the bottom of a large cast-iron skillet. Heat over medium heat until hot. Add steak and sear for 4 to 6 minutes on each side, until the internal temperature reads 130°F for medium-rare. Before the steak reaches desired doneness, add butter and the remaining 2 sprigs of thyme. Baste both sides of the steak with butter until a nice crust develops. Transfer to a plate, then set aside to rest for 6 minutes. The steak should have a nice char with a light pink center.

Assembly Cut the steak against the grain into thick slices. Serve with crawfish sauce on top or on the side.

LOBSTER

1 (1½-lb) lobster

Cajun seasoning, to taste

Salt, to taste

¼ cup (½ stick) butter, room temperature

PASTA

1 tsp olive oil, plus extra for drizzling

10 oz linguine

2 cups heavy cream

4 cloves garlic, chopped

Sprig of thyme

Sprig of rosemary

2 Tbsp Cajun seasoning

1 Tbsp Tony Chachere's Original Creole Seasoning

4 oz lobster claw or tail meat

½ cup grated Parmesan, plus extra for garnish

Juice of ½ lemon

¼ cup (½ stick) butter, room temperature

ASSEMBLY

½ lemon, plus extra wedges to serve

Parsley, for garnish (optional)

Edible flowers, for garnish (optional)

Drago's Pasta

SERVES 2

Chef Austin pays homage to Drago's Restaurant with his adaptation of one of the New Orleans restaurant's signature dishes.

Lobster Preheat oven to 350°F.

With a knife, carefully split lobster in half from head to tail. With your hands, open up lobster all the way and remove the green tomalley and the vein. Season with Cajun seasoning and salt, then add butter. Place lobster on a baking sheet and crack the claws. Bake for 18 minutes, or until tail curls and lobster turns red.

Pasta Meanwhile, bring a large saucepan of salted water to a boil. Add oil and pasta and cook to al dente according to package instructions. Fill a large bowl with ice water. Drain pasta, then shock noodles in the ice bath. Drain again. Drizzle oil over the pasta.

Heat cream in a deep skillet over medium heat. Add garlic, thyme, rosemary, Cajun seasoning, Creole seasoning, and lobster meat and cook for 8 minutes, until it begins to simmer. Stir in Parmesan, lemon juice, and butter. Add pasta and stir to coat. Keep warm.

Assembly Set lobster on a plate. Squeeze lemon juice over the lobster tail, then twist pasta with tongs and place on top of lobster, using it as a boat. Garnish with parsley, Parmesan, and edible flowers (if using). Serve immediately with lemon wedges.

MATSU

▶ OCEANSIDE ◀

CHEF / William Eick

DINING AT Matsu is culinary theater where its dishes take center stage. The dining room is minimalist and serene. On any given evening, when reservations are highly recommended, diners pace through Matsu's ten-course Japanese omakase menu by executive chef and owner William Eick.

As a kid growing up in the Bay Area, Japanese culture permeated his formative years. Japanese tradition is "very minimal and direct and relies heavily on quality ingredients rather than overcomplicated techniques," he shares. The approach to cooking is no different and resonates with him.

For instance, his cabbage gyoza dish transforms most perceptions of the humble vegetable. It's juiced, sautéed, stuffed inside itself, grilled, and topped with caviar. "Why not showcase an ingredient for what it truly can be?" Eick, a longtime Oceanside resident, asks. Then adds, "How can we make one ingredient taste like ten things?"

The restaurant opened in October 2021, though Matsu precedes its permanent brick-and-mortar location. Eick perfected the concept as an occasional, two- to four-seat pop-up within Mission Avenue Bar & Grill, where he was executive chef. "There's a rush that comes from working in a busy restaurant, seeing a guest smile when they enjoy the food, and experiencing the artistry of it all. Every single day, ingredients change and you can prepare it differently and better." For Eick, the challenge is adapting to this constant evolution, and refining his approach to the ingredients while maintaining a consistent high standard for guests. Cooking, restaurants, hospitality—all at once—is everything to him.

SHORT RIBS

4 lbs bone-in or boneless short ribs

10 cloves garlic

2 jalapeños, halved

½ yellow onion, quartered

Bunch of cilantro, plus extra for garnish

2 Tbsp sugar

½ Tbsp red chili flakes

1 cup soy sauce

1 cup white wine

CURRY

1 (13.5-oz) can coconut milk

2 Tbsp panang curry paste

2 Tbsp chopped cilantro

Juice of 1 lime

Salt, to taste

VEGETABLES

20 fingerling potatoes

8 to 10 shiitake mushrooms

2 carrots, halved lengthwise

1 head broccoli, cut into florets

Olive oil, for drizzling

Salt, to taste

Braised Short Rib with Panang Curry and Vegetables

This heart-warming plate of food sings of comfort. William Eick likes to serve it with seasonal vegetables, such as carrots, fingerling potatoes, broccoli, and shiitake mushrooms.

Short ribs Preheat oven to 350°F.

Combine all ingredients in a large roasting pan. Add 3 cups of water and mix well, then cover with aluminum foil and a lid. Braise for 3½ hours, until fork tender.

Curry Meanwhile, bring coconut milk to a boil in a saucepan. Whisk in curry paste, until dissolved. Stir in cilantro and lime juice and set aside for 30 minutes to steep.

Strain sauce, then season to taste with salt. Set aside.

Vegetables In a large bowl, combine all the vegetables, drizzle with oil, season with salt, and mix well. Place in a single layer on a baking sheet and roast for 15 to 20 minutes, until cooked through.

Assembly Spoon curry onto plates. Add vegetables, then place a short rib on top. Garnish with cilantro and serve.

3 lbs pork belly

Sea salt

SHORT-GRAIN RICE

2 cups short-grain rice, such as Koshihikari or Calrose

VIETNAMESE COCONUT CARAMEL GLAZE

2 cloves garlic, smashed

1 to 2 bird's eye chilis, stemmed

½ cup Okinawan brown sugar (see Note)

1 (13.5-oz) can coconut milk

2 Tbsp chopped cilantro stems

2 tsp fish sauce

1 tsp aged shoyu (Japanese soy sauce)

ASSEMBLY

1½ cups Vietnamese Coconut Caramel Glaze (see here), plus extra for drizzling

1 bird's eye chili, thinly sliced, for garnish

1 scallion, thinly sliced, for garnish

Cilantro, mint, and Thai basil leaves, for garnish

Vietnamese Coconut Caramel Pork Belly with Rice

SERVES
6–8

Pork belly Preheat oven to 350°F.

Score the skin of the belly and salt the fat side. Place belly, skin side up, on a roasting rack and roast for 40 minutes. Reduce heat to lowest possible setting and slowly roast for 3½ hours, or until pork is easy to shred. Set aside to rest for 30 minutes. Portion into 5-ounce pieces.

Short-grain rice Meanwhile, wash the rice until water runs clear. Combine rice and 1 cup of water in a bowl and allow to soak for 30 minutes. Cook in rice cooker or per package instructions, until done.

Vietnamese coconut caramel glaze In a saucepan, combine garlic, chili(s), brown sugar, and coconut milk and bring to a boil. Reduce heat to medium-low and simmer for 15 to 20 minutes, until deeply caramelized. Remove from heat and add cilantro stems, then let steep for 15 minutes. Add fish sauce and aged shoyu. Strain. Store leftover caramel glaze in the fridge for up to a week.

Assembly Heat a large skillet over medium-high heat. Add pork belly pieces and sear each side for 2 minutes, until golden brown. Pour coconut caramel glaze into the pan with the meat and heat through.

To serve, spoon rice into a bowl or onto a plate, then add pieces of pork belly. Garnish with chili, scallion, and herbs, then drizzle with more coconut caramel glaze to finish.

***

NOTE Okinawan brown sugar is unrefined, offering a deeper flavor profile compared to other sugars. Source it from online retailers like Amazon or from specialty grocers. Alternatively, any other brown sugar you have on hand will do.

MILONGA
EMPANADAS

▶ *SAN MARCOS* ◀

CHEF + OWNER / Matias Bienati

"**EMPANADAS ARE** like a taco," says Matias Bienati, chef and owner of Milonga Empanadas in San Marcos. "They're so versatile." Yet Bienati, who was born in Buenos Aires, prefers Milonga's signature menu to stay true to the empanada's traditional Argentinian flavors. Flavors include the Criolla, filled with steak, egg, and onion (page 92), and the Caprese, with tomatoes, pesto, and mozzarella, which nods to Argentina's Italian influence. Beyond Milonga's traditional flavors, Bienati harnesses his background as a fine-dining chef at a two-Michelin-starred kitchen in the UK and at Rancho Valencia Resort & Spa in Rancho Santa Fe to air his creativity with seasonal specials, like duck confit with maraschino cherries and pistachios for fall.

Bienati took a detour in business school before enrolling in culinary school. "I was flipping the pancake the hard way," he says of the transition. He attempted to re-create a fine-dining career when he moved back to Argentina from the UK, but it proved challenging due in part to the country's economic climate. He arrived in San Diego in 2016, where his parents were settled.

In 2020, the pandemic gutted the hospitality industry and, like many others, Bienati was forced to pivot. He saw an opportunity to cook as a farmers' market vendor and by 2021 he was preparing lobster rolls, picanha steak sandwiches, and empanadas, which took off. Soon, Bienati was at different markets six times a week, from La Jolla to Rancho Santa Fe to San Marcos. He opened his first brick-and-mortar spot in the summer of 2023, where he serves his freshly baked on demand empanadas alongside Argentinian desserts, like alfajores cookies filled with dulce de leche (page 91).

2/3 cup (1 1/3 sticks) butter, room temperature

1 1/4 cups icing sugar

9 egg yolks

1 tsp vanilla extract

Grated zest of 1 lemon

2 1/2 cups cornstarch

3/4 cup all-purpose flour, plus extra for dusting

1 tsp baking powder

1/2 tsp salt

1 (13.4-oz can) good-quality dulce de leche

Dried coconut flakes, for garnish

Alfajores Cookies

This is a classic South American sandwich cookie, where dulce de leche is sandwiched between shortbread-type biscuits, and then the edges are rolled in coconut flakes.

Cookies In a bowl of a stand mixer fitted with the paddle attachment, cream butter and sugar for 3 minutes, until light and fluffy. Add egg yolks, vanilla, and lemon zest and mix well.

Sift in cornstarch, flour, baking powder, and salt. Slowly mix until everything just comes together. Cover the bowl with plastic wrap and refrigerate for 1 hour.

Preheat oven to 350°F. Line a baking sheet with parchment paper.

Place dough on a clean surface lightly dusted with flour. Using a rolling pin, roll out dough to a 1/3-inch thickness. Using a 3- or 4-inch round cutter, dipped in flour to prevent sticking, cut out rounds.

Place cookie rounds on the prepared baking sheet, evenly spaced 2 inches apart. Bake for 10 minutes, until cooked through but without color. Transfer rounds to a wire rack and set aside to cool completely.

Fill a piping bag with dulce de leche. Add a generous amount of dulce de leche to a cookie round. Place another round on top to sandwich the filling, pressing lightly so the dulce de leche reaches the edges.

Spread the coconut flakes on a plate. Roll the edges of the cookies in coconut. Enjoy!

¼ cup (½ stick) butter

¼ cup lard (divided)

4 medium onions, thinly sliced

1 Tbsp ground cumin

1 Tbsp smoked paprika

2 tsp red chili flakes

3 scallions, chopped, green parts only

¼ cup chopped oregano

Salt and pepper, to taste

1 Tbsp olive oil

1 lb well-marbled beef tri-tip or flap, finely chopped

24 (5-inch) premade empanada disks (see Note)

4 large hard-boiled eggs, finely chopped

½ cup Castelvetrano olives, pitted and finely chopped

Tomato-based yasgua dipping sauce or chimichurri, to serve

Sliced lemons, to serve

Empanada Criolla

MAKES
24
empanadas

This classic empanada sees warm pastry filled with a savory filling made with beef, onion, olives, hard-boiled egg, and an aromatic spice blend. They are quick and easy to make using premade empanada disks.

Empanadas Melt butter and 1 tablespoon of lard in a large nonstick skillet over medium-low heat. Add onions and sauté for 7 to 10 minutes, until translucent. Add cumin, paprika, and chili flakes and cook for another 2 minutes. Remove from heat, then stir in scallion greens and oregano. Season generously with salt and pepper. Transfer to a large bowl.

In the same skillet, heat oil over high heat. Season beef with salt and pepper. Working in batches to avoid overcrowding, add beef to the pan and sauté for 5 minutes. Using a slotted spoon, transfer beef to the onion mixture.

Add the remaining 3 tablespoons of lard to the bowl and mix well. Season to taste with salt and pepper. Cover and chill empanada filling for at least 2 hours but preferably overnight, until firm.

Preheat oven to 400°F. Line a baking sheet with parchment paper.

Place a tablespoon of filling in the center of each empanada disk. Top with the chopped eggs and olives. Using your finger, moisten the edge of each disk with water and fold the dough in half over the filling to form half-moons. Pinch the edges together to seal and crimp, and set on the prepared baking sheet. Bake the empanadas for 15 to 20 minutes, or until dough is golden. Serve with tomato-based yasgua dipping sauce (or chimichurri) and sliced lemons.

NOTE Milonga Empanadas sells premade empanada disks at its San Marcos location, or seek out other brands at your nearest specialty grocer or online.

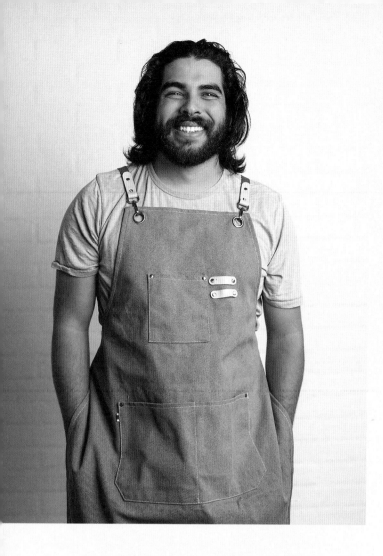

MYSTIC MOCHA

▶ *UNIVERSITY HEIGHTS* ◀

CHEF / Israel Arechiga-Arias

ON ANY GIVEN day, a mix of regulars and University Heights locals flock to Mystic Mocha's bright yellow building. They start their day with alternative-milk lattes named after movie characters, chilaquiles, breakfast burritos, and tacos with homemade guajillo salsas. The coffee shop passed through a few different hands after opening in 2005, before Israel "Izzy" Arechiga-Arias took over as steward in 2020. As a longtime vegan, he offers lots of plant-based breakfast and brunch items that "aren't just a bunch of sides," though there's bacon and chicken for the carnivores, too. Beyond burritos and chilaquiles, Mystic Mocha does breakfast sandwiches with tomato and avocado and sweet and savory plant-based tamales. It's also one of the few places where plant-based milk substitutions, like oat milk, are available at no extra cost.

When Arechiga-Arias acquired the coffee shop after moving back to San Diego from Portland, he had planned to change its name—until two people popped their heads into the space one evening while he was repainting. Turns out, they were Mystic Mocha's original owners, who check up on the shop every now and then. "The place has been important to so many people in the neighborhood," Arechiga-Arias says of the nearly twenty-year-old establishment. So he kept its original name.

The coffee shop is a safe, welcoming place to get some work done with a hot drink or catch up with friends over local craft beer come afternoon. "You can make it what you want it to be," he says. "That's something that we've cultivated and that's worked well."

▶ *Chilaquiles Crudos and Frida Kahlo (Iced Mexican Mocha)*

TOTOPOS

15 (6-inch) corn tortillas

Olive oil, for drizzling

Garlic salt, to taste

Pepper, to taste

SALSA

1 Tbsp olive oil

3 cloves garlic

2 large Roma tomatoes

½ white onion

Juice of 1 orange

1½ tsp veggie bouillon powder

7 dried ancho chiles

Salt, to taste

ASSEMBLY

1 Tbsp olive oil

4 to 6 eggs

3 avocados, peeled and thinly sliced

Cotija cheese

Sour cream

1 yellow onion, finely chopped

Chopped cilantro

Chilaquiles Crudos

SERVES
4–6

According to Israel Arechiga-Arias, these chilaquiles crudos make the perfect hangover (*cruda*) breakfast, but they can also be had for brunch. They are on the smokier side, like the ones he grew up with in Mexico. The salsa is robust enough to stand on its own without the addition of meat.

"At Mystic Mocha, we prepare plant-based options for all our dishes. While these recipes are meant to be vegetarian, you can add bacon, chicken, or chorizo."

Totopos Preheat oven to 375°F.

Stack tortillas and cut them into 4 equal strips. Turn the stack and cut them crosswise into 4. Place tortilla pieces on a baking sheet, then drizzle with oil and season with garlic salt and pepper. Bake for 15 minutes, rotating every 5 minutes, until golden brown.

Salsa Heat oil in a large skillet over medium heat. Add garlic, tomatoes, and onion and sauté for 4 to 5 minutes, until onion edges turn golden. No need to chop up the ingredients here—this step is designed to soften the veggies and bring out the flavors. Any burnt bits will enhance the taste!

Meanwhile, in a saucepan, combine orange juice, veggie bouillon, and 2½ cups of water. Bring to a boil, then add in chiles. Reduce heat to medium-low and simmer for 5 minutes, stirring occasionally, until chiles are softened. Transfer mixture to a blender, add the sautéed veggies, and blend until smooth. Season to taste with salt.

Assembly Heat oil in a large skillet over medium-high heat. Add totopos and salsa and mix until chips are coated. Using tongs, transfer totopos to a serving bowl.

In the same pan, fry the eggs to your liking in the leftover salsa. Portion out the coated chips onto plates and set eggs on top. Top the chilaquiles with avocado, cotija cheese, sour cream, onion, and cilantro.

1 Ibarra Mexican chocolate tablet

2 espresso shots or ½ cup extra-strong coffee

6 to 8 ice cubes

1½ cups unsweetened oat milk

Ground cinnamon, for sprinkling

Whipped cream, for topping (optional)

Frida Kahlo (Iced Mexican Mocha)

SERVES
1

Named after the Mexican icon Frida Kahlo, this chocolate- and cinnamon-tinged iced coffee is one of Mystic Mocha's best-selling drinks. "It's important that our drinks and recipes can be vegan to reflect my roots. Here, we use Ibarra Mexican chocolate, which only has four ingredients—cacao, sugar, cinnamon, and soy," says owner Izzy Arechiga-Arias. "Mexican mochas are a simple yet delicious way to start a San Diego morning."

Mocha Using a grater, grate the chocolate tablet to make 3 tablespoons chocolate shavings. In a pint glass, whisk together espresso (or coffee) and 2 tablespoons chocolate shavings, until thoroughly mixed.

Add ice and fill with oat milk. Sprinkle with cinnamon and 1 tablespoon chocolate shavings. Top with whipped cream (if using).

NECTARINE GROVE

▶ *ENCINITAS* ◀

CHEF / Rhiana Glor

CLICHÉS PERSIST because we turn to them time and again. So, if necessity is the mother of invention, as they say, Rhiana Glor's plunge into restaurant ownership begins here.

In 2006, Glor was a newly minted San Diegan who fell in love with coastal Encinitas. At the time, it was difficult to find organic or gluten-free eats in the area.

To satisfy her own palate for the kind of health-conscious food she grew to love in her hometown of Santa Cruz, and with her mom's encouragement, Glor opened not one, but two places that offer the myriad flavors she explored while living in Australia. "I was bursting with food ideas," Glor says. Her first, Healthy Creations Cafe, specialized in plant-based bowls and sustainable meat options.

In 2018, she opened Nectarine Grove in Leucadia and followed it up with another branch in Del Mar. Since then, the popular daytime spot has blossomed into a destination for people with allergies or food intolerances. "We are gluten-free, we have dairy-free options, and we cook with avocado oil," Glor says. Regardless of dietary preferences and needs, Nectarine Grove's regulars come for the food, like its top-selling carne asada burrito with grass-fed beef and superfood lattes bolstered with collagen. They stay to get work done and linger over its local gluten-free beers and hard kombuchas on tap. "I didn't anticipate opening anything when I moved back from Australia, but I saw a need and decided to put my nutritional knowledge and love of healthy food to work." Now, it's hard to imagine Encinitas without a spot like it.

▶ *Plantain-Crusted Fried Chicken and Waffles with Honey Mustard Sauce*

WAFFLES

1½ cups + 2 Tbsp milk or dairy-free milk

1 tsp lemon juice

2 eggs, separated

1⅓ cups brown rice flour

⅔ cup + 2 Tbsp tapioca flour

½ cup sorghum flour

3 Tbsp coconut sugar

2 tsp baking powder

1 tsp psyllium husk

¼ tsp sea salt

½ cup avocado oil or other light-flavored oil

2 tsp vanilla extract

HONEY MUSTARD SAUCE

½ cup mayonnaise

5 Tbsp stone-ground mustard

5 Tbsp honey

2 Tbsp avocado oil

2 tsp apple cider vinegar

1½ tsp lemon juice

PLANTAIN-CRUSTED FRIED CHICKEN

3 cups plantain chips (180 g)

3 Tbsp tapioca flour

1 tsp sea salt

¾ tsp paprika

½ tsp ground mustard

½ tsp onion powder

¼ tsp smoked paprika

1 egg

1½ Tbsp hot sauce

2 large chicken breasts

Avocado oil, for frying

Plantain-Crusted Fried Chicken and Waffles with Honey Mustard Sauce

SERVES

4

This flavorful dish sees a classic marriage of crisp fried chicken and cake-like waffles topped with lashings of honey mustard sauce. And it's gluten-free.

Waffles Preheat a waffle maker.

In a small bowl, combine milk and lemon juice and set aside.

In the bowl of a stand mixer fitted with the whisk attachment (or using a hand mixer), whip egg whites until stiff peaks form.

Meanwhile, combine flours, coconut sugar, baking powder, psyllium husk, and salt in a large bowl. Mix in egg yolks, milk with lemon juice, oil, and vanilla, until smooth. Gently stir in whipped egg whites.

Pour a cup of batter into the hot waffle iron and cook for 3 minutes, regardless of the ready light on the waffle iron, until waffles are slightly browned on top. Transfer to a plate. Make 3 more waffles. Keep warm.

Honey mustard sauce Whisk all ingredients together.

Plantain-crusted fried chicken Place plantain chips in a food processor and process to small crumbs. (It's okay to have a few bigger pieces.) Transfer to a plate.

In a small bowl, combine tapioca flour, salt, paprika, ground mustard, onion powder, and smoked paprika. Transfer to a plate.

In another small bowl, whisk together egg, hot sauce, and 1 tablespoon of water.

Maple syrup, for drizzling
Knobs of butter

Place a chicken breast on a cutting board and halve it lengthwise, placing one hand on top of the breast and using the other to guide the knife through it. You will have 2 thin breasts. Repeat with the other chicken breast so you have 4 thin halves.

To bread the chicken, dip a piece into the spiced flour mixture, then the egg mixture, then the plantain crumbs. Repeat with the remaining chicken. (You can prepare the chicken to this point ahead of time and refrigerate for 1 to 2 days.) Set aside.

Heat 1 inch of oil in a deep skillet over medium-high heat, until the temperature of the oil reaches 350°F. Gently lower a piece of breaded chicken into the pan. Cook for 2 minutes, then flip and cook for another 1 to 2 minutes, until the internal temperature reaches 160°F.

Transfer chicken to a paper towel–lined plate to drain. Repeat with the remaining chicken.

Assembly Place waffles on plates. Slice chicken into strips and set on top of the waffles. Drizzle with honey mustard sauce and maple syrup and top with butter. Enjoy!

VANILLA-ALMOND CRUST

⅔ cup blanched almond flour

⅔ cup sweet white rice flour

⅓ cup tapioca flour

3 Tbsp organic cane sugar

⅛ tsp sea salt

7 Tbsp (¾ stick + 1 Tbsp) salted butter, cubed and chilled

1 tsp vanilla extract

LEMON CREAM CHEESE FILLING

1 (8-oz) package cream cheese

½ cup organic cane sugar

⅓ cup heavy cream

1 tsp vanilla extract

½ tsp lemon juice, plus extra if needed

½ tsp lemon zest

ASSEMBLY

2 cups fruit, such as berries, kiwi, mandarin orange slices, or grapes, sliced

2 Tbsp apricot jam, for glaze (optional)

Fruit Tart with Vanilla-Almond Crust and Lemon Cream Cheese

SERVES 6–8

Chef Glor recommends placing one type of fruit along the border and building concentric circles of different fruit towards the center.

Any round pan will do, but it should have a removable bottom to help ease the tart from the pan.

Vanilla-almond crust In the bowl of a stand mixer fitted with the paddle attachment, combine flours, sugar, and salt and gently mix. Add cold butter cubes and vanilla and mix on medium speed, until a dough ball forms.

Place dough into a 9-inch round tart pan with a removable bottom. Press it into the sides and bottom, until the pan is entirely covered. Using a fork, prick holes into the base. Freeze for 20 minutes.

Meanwhile, preheat oven to 350°F.

Bake the tart crust for 20 minutes, or until golden brown. Set aside to cool.

Lemon cream cheese filling In the bowl of a stand mixer fitted with the whisk attachment (or using a hand mixer), whisk cream cheese and sugar until smooth. Slowly mix in cream, vanilla, and lemon juice and zest. Taste and add more lemon juice if desired. Chill in the refrigerator until crust is completely cool.

Assembly Pour the filling into the crust. Arrange fruit decoratively on top.

In a small bowl, combine jam (if using) and 1 tablespoon of hot water to thin it out. Using a pastry brush, brush the glaze over the fruit, if desired. This gives the fruit a glossy appearance and extends its freshness. Chill the tart until ready to serve.

ORFILA WINERY TASTING ROOM & KITCHEN

▶ *OCEANSIDE* ◀

CHEF / Luke Morganstern

ORFILA WINERY'S tasting room and restaurant in downtown Oceanside, just steps from the city's sand and surf, is a unique way to sample some of the region's local wine and tuck into a meal. Executive chef Luke Morganstern noticed the area's palm trees first when he arrived in Oceanside from upstate New York, sight unseen. As the tasting room's inaugural chef, he infuses its menu with Mediterranean flavors and vegetable-forward dishes inspired by his parents' vegetarian restaurant, which he helped out at as a teen and young adult.

Orfila's menu is stacked with share plates, from smashed Japanese sweet potatoes with ponzu aioli to grilled lamb chops to surf-and-turf entrées. Morganstern's affinity for health-conscious eating has crept into the menu as well, with a generous use of spices, herbs, citrus, and olive oil for flavor. Pretzels are dusted with za'atar and served with Merlot beer cheese, and his grilled-to-order octopus with chorizo and Calabrian chili succotash continues to be a best-seller. "It's light, not too complicated, and just delicious," he says. Orfila's vegan coconut cake, a family recipe, makes a sweet final act to a meal.

The menu pairs perfectly with their award-winning wines, including French and Italian varietals, and those produced with grapes from Sonoma, San Luis Obispo, and Santa Barbara Counties. (All of which can be sampled at their Escondido winery.) And whether dining inside or on the plant-filled side patio, guests come as they are, whether elegant or ultra-casual. "Maybe you were just at the beach, and you've got a T-shirt, shorts, and sandals on," Morganstern says. It's all good!

CAKE

Olive oil, for greasing

3 cups all-purpose flour

2 cups sugar

1 cup raw coconut flakes

2 tsp baking soda

Grated zest of 2 lemons

Grated zest of 2 limes

Grated zest of 2 oranges

1 cup coconut milk

1 tsp vanilla extract

4 tsp apple cider vinegar

TOASTED COCONUT FLAKES

1½ cups raw coconut flakes

VEGAN BUTTERCREAM FROSTING

1 lb vegan butter, such as Earth Balance, set aside at room temperature for 10 minutes

3½ cups confectioners' sugar

1 tsp vanilla extract

½ tsp ground cinnamon

Vegan Citrus Coconut Cake

SERVES
8–12

Cake Preheat oven to 375°F. Grease two (8-inch) round cake pans.

In a large bowl, combine flour, sugar, coconut flakes, baking soda, and citrus zests. Mix well.

In a separate bowl, combine coconut milk, vanilla, and 1 cup of water. Mix wet ingredients into dry until batter is smooth. Stir in vinegar.

Divide batter between the prepared cake pans. Bake for 20 minutes, or until golden and a toothpick inserted into the center of the cake comes out clean. Set aside at room temperature to cool for at least 30 minutes.

Toasted coconut flakes Preheat oven to 350°F.

Lay out coconut flakes in a single layer on a baking sheet. Bake for 5 minutes, until golden brown and fragrant. Check frequently as they can burn quickly. (Alternatively, toast coconut flakes in a skillet over medium-low heat for 3 minutes.) Set aside to cool.

Vegan buttercream frosting Combine all ingredients in the bowl of a stand mixer fitted with the whisk attachment and whisk until smooth.

Assembly Using a knife or spatula, scrape around the sides of the cakes. Invert one cake layer onto the serving plate of your choice. With a rubber spatula, scoop a third of the frosting onto the cake and spread evenly.

Lay second cake layer on top. Spread the rest of the frosting over the top and sides of the cake. Cover cake with toasted coconut flakes, lightly patting them into the frosting with one hand.

Slice and enjoy!

OCTOPUS

2 Tbsp canola and olive oil blend (divided)

5 cloves garlic, chopped

2 stalks celery, sliced

1 small yellow onion, chopped

1 carrot, chopped

Sprig of thyme

Sprig of rosemary

½ tsp salt

¼ tsp pepper

Juice of 2 lemons

1 cup red wine

1 (3- to 5-lb) octopus

ARUGULA SALAD

½ lb smoked bacon

4 cups arugula

1 red onion, sliced

1 lb cherry tomatoes, halved

Juice of 2 lemons

2 Tbsp aged balsamic vinegar

1 tsp olive oil

Salt and pepper, to taste

ASSEMBLY

Lemon juice, to taste

Microgreens, for garnish (optional)

Seared Octopus with Arugula Salad

SERVES
4

Octopus Heat 1 tablespoon oil in a large heavy-bottomed stockpot over medium heat. Add garlic, celery, onion, carrot, thyme, and rosemary and sauté for 10 minutes, until onion is softened and translucent. Add salt, pepper, and lemon juice. Pour in wine and deglaze. Add 4 quarts of water and bring to a boil.

Carefully dip the octopus tentacles in seven times, which tenderizes the flesh and helps the tentacles to curl, then gently lower octopus into the water. Reduce heat to medium-low and cover. Simmer for 3 hours.

Transfer the cooked octopus to a large plate and refrigerate for 30 minutes, until cool to the touch. Slice off the head at its base and discard, then remove the beak. Then cut through to divide tentacles into 8 pieces.

Arugula salad Preheat oven to 350°F.

Place bacon on a baking sheet and bake for 10 minutes, until crispy. Transfer bacon to a paper towel–lined plate to drain. Slice into small pieces.

In a large bowl, combine bacon and the remaining ingredients and mix well.

Assembly Heat the remaining tablespoon of oil in a large cast-iron skillet over high heat. Add the tentacles and fry for a minute per side, until seared.

Transfer arugula salad to a serving platter. Arrange seared octopus on top. Squeeze lemon juice over the pieces. Garnish with microgreens (if using) and serve immediately.

PARAKEET CAFÉ

▶ *CORONADO, DEL MAR,*
LA JOLLA, LITTLE ITALY ◀

CHEF / Miguel Arévalo

SEVENTEEN YEARS ago, Carol Roizen and her husband, Jonathan, moved from Mexico City to La Jolla, California, to start a new life in the States after their second daughter, Michelle, was diagnosed with a rare disease when she was just four months old. To better support her, Roizen shifted gears from her practice in law to study nutritional health and food. "It offered us a semblance of control amidst the uncertainty," she says. When her daughter's iron count dipped due to weekly blood draws, she would prepare baby food with loads of spinach and beans. "The next week, her counts would be much better."

While Michelle underwent chemotherapy for three years, Roizen completed programs with the Institute for Integrative Nutrition and Le Cordon Bleu and received a master's in spiritual psychology from the University of Santa Monica. And together, Carol and Jonathan explored nutrition through juicing and a plant-based, organic, whole-foods diet. These paths are reflected in Parakeet Café's menu, which is overseen by executive chef Miguel Arévalo. Bakery director Quentin Collignon leads its pastry program.

"My commitment is to high-quality food and to crafting something that's full of color, flavor, and texture," Roizen says. Whether at Parakeet's original location in La Jolla, where Arévalo started as a line cook, or their other locations across San Diego, Orange, and Los Angeles Counties, look for lattes infused with adaptogens like spirulina or ashwagandha, an array of baked goods, and beautiful breakfast, lunch, and dinner dishes. And the focus is on making everything in house: from "syrups and dressings to caramelized onions that caramelize for eight hours," Arévalo says. Parakeet's golden goddess salad has been a hit since they first opened their doors in 2017. There are also dishes inspired by Roizen's Mexican heritage, like the All I Avo Wanted. "It's a cross between avocado toast and a Mexican *sope*," she says.

1 cup toasted cashews

1 morita chile pepper (see Note)

¼ cup garlic cloves

1 Tbsp kosher salt

1 tsp pepper

¼ tsp coriander seeds

2 Tbsp lemon juice

2 Tbsp tahini

2 Tbsp sesame oil

Zest of 1 lemon

SALAD

1 cup broccoli florets

1 cup Brussels sprouts, trimmed and halved

1 bulb fennel, cut into ½-inch cubes (1 cup)

1 sweet potato, cut into ½-inch cubes (1 cup)

¼ cup extra-virgin olive oil

Salt and pepper, to taste

2 cups baby kale

½ cup toasted almonds

½ cup radish sprouts

½ cup pomegranate seeds

Winter Salad

"Roasted vegetables dance with smoky notes, meeting the crisp embrace of baby kale. Crowned with a creamy vegan tahini and morita dressing, this dish is a vibrant medley of texture and color and a harmonious blend of Mexican and Mediterranean flavors," says executive chef Mike Arévalo, the creator of this delicious salad.

Tahini and morita dressing Combine all ingredients in a blender. Pour in 1 cup of water and blend for 3 minutes, until smooth.

Salad Preheat oven to 350°F.

In a large bowl, combine broccoli, Brussels sprouts, fennel, and sweet potato. Add oil, salt, and pepper and toss to coat. Spread out on a baking sheet and roast for 15 minutes.

In a bowl, combine roasted vegetables, kale, and ½ cup of dressing and toss to mix. Transfer to a serving bowl. Top with toasted almonds, radish sprouts, and pomegranate seeds.

NOTE *Beautifully pigmented in purple-red, morita chile peppers are dried and smoked red jalapeños. They are available whole or crushed at Mexican markets, specialty grocers, or online.*

ROASTED CARPACCIO
PINEAPPLE

10 cilantro leaves

2 pods cardamom

2½ cups sugar

2 Tbsp black peppercorns

1 pineapple, sliced into
 thin wedges

VANILLA FINANCIERS

¾ cup (1½ sticks) butter,
 plus extra for greasing

5 cups almond flour

⅓ cup all-purpose flour

8 eggs

2 cups honey

1 Tbsp vanilla extract

Vanilla Financiers with
Roasted Carpaccio Pineapple

MAKES
6–8
financiers

"The almond-infused goodness of the cake is complemented by the caramelized sweetness of tender pineapple," says bakery director Quentin Collignon of his dessert.

Roasted carpaccio pineapple Preheat oven to 375°F.

In a large baking dish, combine all ingredients except pineapple. Pour in 2½ quarts of water and mix well. Add pineapple wedges. Cover with aluminum foil and pierce the top with a fork to release steam. Bake for 30 to 35 minutes, until pineapple wedges are softened. Set aside to cool for 30 minutes. Drain pineapple, reserving the braising liquid. Pour roasted pineapple juice into a pitcher and refrigerate.

Vanilla financiers Preheat oven to 350°F. Grease a six- to eight-portion financier pan.

Melt butter in a saucepan over medium-low heat, until browned. Set aside to cool slightly.

Combine both flours in a bowl. Using a spatula, slowly pour the lukewarm brown butter into the bowl and mix until fully incorporated. Mix in eggs, honey, and vanilla. Pour batter into the prepared pan and bake for 15 to 20 minutes, until golden brown. Set aside for 15 minutes to cool.

Assembly Remove financiers from the pan. Place slightly warm pineapple wedges over financiers.

Serve the financiers and roasted carpaccio pineapple with glasses of the chilled juice.

PETITE MADELINE BAKERY

▶ *OCEANSIDE* ◀

CHEF + OWNER (R) Christine Loyola
MANAGER (L) Rachel Moreno

FOR MORE than fifteen years, Petite Madeline has gifted the Oceanside community with fresh croissants, desserts, and other scratch-baked goodies. "We have no margarine back there!" chef-owner Christine Loyola declares, nodding toward the kitchen. The same goes for its breakfast and lunch menus, where home-made hollandaise graces its Benedicts and the ever-popular savory crepe with chicken and mushrooms. Produce from local farms, namely Cyclops Farms in Fallbrook, is also a common recurrence.

During the massive layoffs that accompanied the stock market crash in the late 1990s, Loyola took a severance from her finance job and rein-vented herself. She enrolled in culinary school, inspired by the Bay Area's gourmet culture. As an intern at the famed Chez Panisse in Berkeley, Loyola learned the value of quality ingredients, then dove into artisan laminates at La Farine Bakery. After visiting her brother in San Diego County, she uncovered an opportunity to apply her culinary expertise in Oceanside. Despite taking a risk as a self-described latecomer to the restaurant industry (Loyola was in her mid-forties at the time), she grew Petite Madeline into the go-to daytime spot in Oceanside.

Her team has since expanded to include her daughter Rachel Moreno, who manages the front of house. Throughout the week, guests slide into the eatery's wide booths in a welcoming space on the corner of North Coast Highway and Pier View Way. They're surrounded by high ceilings, long mirrors, and natural light. "People love the atmosphere, the family-feel," Moreno says. "It's what represents us most."

▶ *Crispy Eggs Flamenco*

TOMATO SAUCE

2 (28-oz) cans whole San Marzano tomatoes, with juices (5½ cups)

1 Tbsp olive oil

1 yellow onion, finely chopped

1 bay leaf

3 cloves garlic, thinly sliced

Salt and pepper, to taste

SOFT POLENTA

¼ cup extra-virgin olive oil

½ Tbsp kosher salt, plus extra to taste

1 cup polenta or yellow cornmeal

¼ cup (½ stick) butter, cut into cubes

¼ cup grated Parmigiano-Reggiano, plus extra to taste

Pepper, to taste

SUCCOTASH

2 cups baby lima beans, peeled

1 Tbsp olive oil

½ onion, chopped

½ red bell pepper, seeded, deveined, and chopped

3 cloves garlic, finely chopped

2 to 3 ears fresh corn, kernels shaved

Salt and pepper, to taste

1 Tbsp white wine vinegar

2 Tbsp finely chopped cilantro, plus extra for garnish

Crispy Eggs Flamenco

SERVES 4

The panko crust lends texture to soft eggs, while succotash and polenta with tomato sauce act as savory and crunchy counterpoints. If you prefer, the succotash can be replaced with your favorite side salad.

To save time, you can also use store-bought marinara sauce instead of making homemade tomato sauce. Just thin it out with some water and warm through before use.

Tomato sauce Put tomatoes into a large bowl and crush with your hands. Pour 1 cup of water into one can and then the other, sloshing it around to get the last of the tomato juices. Add to the crushed tomatoes. Set aside.

Heat oil in a large skillet over medium heat. Add onion and bay leaf and sauté for 5 minutes. Add garlic and sauté for another 1 to 2 minutes, until onion is softened and translucent. Add crushed tomatoes and simmer for 5 minutes. Season to taste with salt and pepper. Remove bay leaf.

Soft polenta Bring 4½ cups of water to a boil in a medium saucepan. Add oil and salt, then reduce heat to medium and simmer. Whisk in polenta in a steady stream, until smooth and incorporated. Reduce heat to medium-low and simmer for 20 to 25 minutes, until polenta is creamy.

Remove pan from the heat, then whisk in butter and Parmigiano-Reggiano. Season with salt and pepper, then add more cheese to taste. Set aside.

Succotash Bring a saucepan of water to a boil. Add lima beans and cook for 3 minutes. Reduce heat to medium-low, cover, and simmer for 15 minutes, until soft. Drain, then set aside.

Heat oil in a skillet over medium heat. Add onion and bell pepper and sauté for 5 to 7 minutes, until onion is translucent. Add garlic and sauté for another minute, until fragrant. Stir in corn and cook for 3 to 4 minutes, until it is just cooked but still has a slight crunch. Season to taste with salt and pepper. Add

EGGS

9 eggs (divided)
2 cups all-purpose flour
2 cups panko breadcrumbs
8 cups vegetable oil, for frying
Salt, to taste

cooked lima beans and vinegar. Simmer for 2 to 3 minutes to blend flavors. Mix in cilantro. Keep warm over low heat.

Eggs Bring a small saucepan of water to a boil. Add 8 whole eggs and boil for 4 to 5 minutes. Using a slotted spoon, transfer to a bowl of cold water to stop the cooking. Remove from cold water, then dry with a paper towel and gently peel off shells.

Beat the remaining egg in a small bowl. Place flour and panko in separate shallow bowls. Dip a soft-boiled egg into flour to coat, then into the beaten egg. Gently roll egg in panko bread-crumbs. Repeat with remaining soft-boiled eggs.

Heat oil in a heavy saucepan over medium-high heat. Add eggs and deep fry for 30 seconds to a minute, until golden. Work in batches, if necessary, to avoid overcrowding. Drain on a paper towel–lined plate, then sprinkle with a little salt.

Assembly Ladle large spoonfuls of soft polenta onto serving plates. Spoon tomato sauce over the polenta and top with succotash. Carefully set 2 crispy eggs on top of each serving. Garnish with cilantro.

Nonstick cooking spray
3 cups (6 sticks) butter, softened
2 cups cake flour, sifted
2 cups confectioners' sugar

Meltaways

MAKES
30–35
cookies

"This melt-in-your-mouth cookie is delicious and so easy to make!!!" says Christine Loyola. "When I was asked to demonstrate a recipe to a grade-school class, I chose this recipe because this best-seller has just three ingredients. A stand mixer will do all the work of aerating the dough."

Cookies Preheat oven to 350°F. Lightly spray a baking sheet with cooking spray.

Combine the remaining ingredients in the bowl of a stand mixer fitted with the paddle attachment. Beat on low speed until slightly mixed. Increase to high speed and beat for another 5 to 8 minutes, until fluffy.

Using a rubber spatula, transfer dough into a piping bag fitted with a large star tip. Fill the piping bag only halfway so that you can twist the top of the bag. Pipe dough into 3-inch rosettes or shell shapes (putting pressure on the first squeeze then tapering as you shape) on the prepared baking sheet, evenly spaced 2 inches apart. Bake for 7 minutes, then turn the pan 180 degrees and bake for another 6 to 7 minutes, until golden. Set aside to cool.

PIZZA CASSETTE

▶ *MORENA* ◀

CHEF / Jimmy Terwilliger

CHEF AND owner Jimmy Terwilliger opened Pizza Cassette in 2022, nearly a decade after honing his wood-fired pizza skills at Catania in La Jolla. At Pizza Cassette, the open kitchen is an infernal performance that dazzles guests young and old. All are mesmerized by its oven—the star of the show—firing at over 800°F. "It's primitive and fast," Terwilliger says of fire-fueled cooking.

When it comes to whipping up pizza combinations and other specials, sometimes the music comes first, other times it's the food. Red and white pies (A sides and B sides, respectively) are driven by seasonality and Terwilliger's musical tastes. If southern California was a pizza, it'd be Pizza Cassette's Lemon Song (page 122). It features local spinach, thinly sliced farmers' market lemons, fresh ground house-made pork sausage, fresh mozzarella, and ricotta. "We have all these flavors year-round," Terwilliger says, in a nod to San Diego's long growing season.

Before Pizza Cassette opened where it stands today, nestled in The Gärten in Morena, Terwilliger originally pursued a brick-and-mortar space. It came with old deck ovens capable of only churning out rectangular pizzas, so he had planned to do just that. Cassette, meaning "case" in Italian, refers to the boxes the dough is stored in at traditional Neapolitan pizzerias. While the brick-and-mortar location fell through, the name stuck.

BACON JAM

½ lb bacon, diced

½ onion, chopped

½ cup balsamic vinegar

¼ cup brown sugar

1 Tbsp olive oil

1 Tbsp mustard seeds

½ Tbsp salt

1 tsp pepper

BALSAMIC REDUCTION

2 cups balsamic vinegar (see Note)

PIZZA

1 quantity Pizza Dough (page 122)

Canola oil, for greasing

¼ cup Bacon Jam (see here)

⅔ cup cubed mozzarella

¼ cup cherry tomatoes, quartered

¼ cup grated Parmesan

1 cup arugula

Pork Soda Pizza

MAKES
2
(12-inch) pizzas

Bacon jam Brown bacon in a large skillet over medium-high heat. Transfer bacon to a paper towel–lined plate to drain. Remove excess fat from skillet. Add bacon and onion and sauté over medium heat for 7 minutes, until onion is translucent.

Add the remaining ingredients and ¼ cup of water. Cook for 20 minutes, stirring occasionally, until most of the liquid has evaporated. Set aside to cool.

Balsamic reduction Pour balsamic vinegar into a saucepan and simmer over medium heat for 15 minutes, until thick, glossy, and reduced by a third. It should easily coat a spoon. Set aside to cool to room temperature. Leftover balsamic reduction can be stored in a dark space for up to 6 months.

Pizza Preheat oven to 500°F.

Place your prepared pizza rounds on a lightly oiled baking sheet. Top with cooled bacon jam, then scatter with mozzarella cubes. Add tomatoes and Parmesan. Bake for 5 to 7 minutes, until crispy.

Top pizzas with arugula and a drizzle of balsamic reduction and serve immediately.

NOTE *Seek out a good-quality balsamic vinegar, such as one from Modena or Reggio Emilia, for this reduction.*

PIZZA DOUGH

1⅓ cups room-temperature water (divided)

½ tsp active dry yeast

4 cups "00" flour, all-purpose flour, or bread flour (divided), plus extra for dusting

2½ tsp sea salt

ASSEMBLY

Canola oil, for greasing

1 cup cooked ground pork sausage

2 cups baby spinach

⅔ cup cubed mozzarella

¼ cup ricotta

¼ cup grated Parmesan

1 Sorrento lemon, seeded and thinly sliced

Citrus flowers or other edible florals, for garnish

Lemon Song Pizza

MAKES
2
(12-inch) pizzas

Pizza dough Pour 1¼ cups of the water into the bowl of a stand mixer fitted with the hook attachment. Stir in yeast. Add 3½ cups flour. Mix on the lowest speed for 2 minutes. Add salt and the remaining water and ½ cup flour and mix again on the lowest speed for 3 minutes. Increase to high speed and mix for 30 seconds, or until dough forms a ball and is slightly sticky to the touch.

Remove dough from dough hook and leave in the mixing bowl. Cover bowl with a damp towel or oiled plastic wrap. Do not wrap it airtight as the dough needs to breathe. Set aside to rest for 6 to 8 hours at room temperature.

Set dough on a lightly floured surface. Using a knife or a bench scraper, divide dough in half. Carefully roll dough into smooth, round balls. Be sure to close the dough balls on the bottom as best you can so as not to create thin spots when you stretch them. Place dough balls in a covered container and set aside to rest for another 4 to 8 hours at room temperature.

Transfer dough balls to a lightly floured surface and carefully stretch into 12-inch disks. Dough should remain slightly sticky yet easy to handle during the entire process after mixing. If the dough seems too sticky or is hard to work with, add a bit of flour.

Assembly Preheat oven to 500°F.

Place your prepared pizza rounds on a lightly oiled baking sheet. Top with pork sausage and spinach. Scatter with mozzarella cubes, then add ricotta and Parmesan evenly across the pizzas. Finally, arrange lemon slices on top. Bake for 5 to 7 minutes, until crispy. Garnish with citrus flowers (or other edible florals) and enjoy!

PONTO LAGO

▶ *CARLSBAD* ◀

CHEF / Pierre Albaladejo

PIERRE ALBALADEJO has cheffed in some of the most picturesque coastal locales in the world, from Monterey to Maui, Barcelona to Carlsbad, though his earliest seaside memories took hold along the Atlantic coast. As a child growing up in a tiny village in France's Basque region, farm-to-table cooking was a necessity. At the time, the town lacked a grocery store. "[We'd] go to the Saturday farmers' market to get our produce for the week and to the harbor to pick up the fish for the day," he says.

Now in Carlsbad, as executive chef of Park Hyatt Aviara (where he's been for twenty years), Albaladejo oversees three restaurants, including Ponto Lago. Its menu of wood-fire-grilled seafood specialties and raw bar offerings—oysters, ceviches, aguachiles—draws on its proximity to the ocean and Mexico's Baja peninsula. For weekend brunch, *asado* (grilled meats), concha French toast, and agave-based cocktails keep with the theme. South American flavors also make their way into dishes, like the bone-in strip steak with red chimichurri; while the crowd-pleasing Ensenada striped bass with chilis and garlic is an interpretation of a traditional dish popular in the Basque region.

Guests settle into cushy banquettes in the coastal modern dining room, with floor-to-ceiling windows that look out toward the Pacific and center around Ponto Lago's open-face kitchen. Here, Albaladejo prefers understated preparations so the region's fresh bounty shines. "We're working ahead of anyone else in the country as far as seasonality. That's a big asset for a chef," he says.

BAJA COCKTAIL SAUCE

2½ cups fresh tomato juice

1 cup clam juice

¾ cup lime juice

2 Tbsp Worcestershire sauce, plus extra to taste

1 Tbsp + 2 tsp celery salt, plus extra to taste

2 tsp dried chiltepín chiles, plus extra to taste (see Note)

1 tsp pepper, plus extra to taste

POACHED SHRIMP

2 Tbsp lime juice

2 Tbsp salt

30 (16/20) white Mexican shrimp, peeled and deveined

ASSEMBLY

3 cups Baja Cocktail Sauce (see here)

1 red onion, thinly sliced (¾ cup)

½ cucumber, diced (1 cup)

Salt, to taste

2 avocados, peeled, pitted, and chopped

6 Tbsp whole cilantro leaves

Baja Shrimp Cocktail

SERVES
4–6

Mexican shrimp are gently poached, then marinated in a flavorful cocktail sauce, for this tasty appetizer that goes hand-in-hand with ice-cold Modelo.

Baja cocktail sauce Combine all ingredients in a blender and blend until smooth. Season to taste with more Worcestershire sauce, salt, pepper, and chiles. If desired, pass through a fine-mesh sieve for an even smoother sauce. Refrigerate until needed.

NOTE *Chiltepín chiles may look like tiny red berries, but these peppers pack a bold, spicy kick. Find them fresh or dried at Mexican markets, specialty grocers, or online.*

Poached shrimp In a saucepan, combine 2 quarts of cold water with the lime juice and salt and bring to a boil. Add shrimp and cook over medium-high heat, stirring occasionally, until shrimp are just cooked through and temperature reaches 170°F on an instant-read thermometer, about 4 to 7 minutes (do not exceed this temperature). Drain shrimp, then rinse under cold running water. Drain well.

Assembly In a bowl, combine shrimp, cocktail sauce, red onion, and cucumber. Season to taste with salt. Transfer to a deep serving dish, then top with avocado and cilantro. Serve immediately.

2 red bell peppers

1½ cups olive oil, plus extra for greasing

4 (1-lb) whole branzinos or red snappers, cleaned

Salt and pepper, to taste

5 cloves garlic, sliced

1 Tbsp thinly sliced dried guajillo chile

6 Tbsp sherry vinegar

24 cherry tomatoes, halved

⅓ cup Italian parsley leaves

2 Tbsp capers

Branzino Espagnol

SERVES
4

"This simple yet delectable dish is rooted in my beloved Basque Country," says Pierre Albaladejo. "It's a Baja California play on a classic dish and a culinary expression of my origin."

Branzino Preheat a grill over high heat. Add bell peppers and grill for 3 minutes until all sides are charred. Transfer peppers to a bowl and cover with plastic wrap. Set aside for 5 minutes. Peel, remove seeds, and cut into thin strips.

Keep the grill heated over medium-high heat and oil grates. Season whole fish with salt and pepper. Add to the grill and grill for 5 minutes, until skin is nicely caramelized and crispy. Flip over and cook for another 5 minutes, or until desired doneness. Place fish in a deep serving platter.

Heat oil in a large skillet over medium heat. Add garlic and sauté for 1 minute, until lightly brown. Add chile and cook for another minute. Remove from heat and set aside to cool for 3 minutes before stirring in sherry vinegar (to avoid excess splatter).

Add tomatoes, parsley, capers, and bell pepper strips. Season with salt and pepper. Bring to a boil.

Pour hot sauce over the fish and serve immediately.

THE PRIVATEER
COAL FIRE PIZZA

▶ *OCEANSIDE* ◀

OWNER (L) Charlie Anderson

GENERAL MANAGER (C) Sage Anderson

CHEF (R) Oscar Garcia

THE PRIVATEER Coal Fire Pizza doesn't just do pizzas, although their extensive pie menu (with many named after neighboring action sports businesses) is a draw. The pizzas, like their other Italian, Mexican, and Californian-inflected items, from pastas to salads, feature fresh ingredients from their neighbors. "We are so fortunate that we have four farms up the street (Palmquist Elementary, Lincoln Middle School, South Oceanside Elementary, and Cyclops Farms) that produce a percentage of our organic veggies and herbs," says owner Charlie Anderson. Charlie opened The Privateer with his best friend, Jamey, in 2012.

Sage Anderson, Charlie's son, oversees the restaurant and marketplace. "Oceanside has given me everything I have—the restaurant, my family, my friends, my wife grew up down the street from me," Sage says of his South Oceanside roots. Oscar Garcia, who has been with The Privateer for eight years and got his start in the restaurant world at fifteen, is its chef. "I found myself on a hot summer night learning to sauté and I fell in love with the rush and intensity of the heat, the fast-paced work, and the gratification of making delicious food that people enjoyed," Garcia, from nearby Carlsbad, remembers.

The Privateer is located in a former 7-Eleven off South Coast Highway, and its guests gather in the local art–filled dining area or in the wine shop next door. They enjoy pizzas like the Brixton, with Grana Padano and lemon zest ricotta, a *Wine Spectator*-awarded wine list, plus regular live music and comedy nights. And wine dinners—a collaboration between Garcia and Level 1 sommelier Susan Porter-Guarino. "We're independently owned, locally supported, family operated," Sage says.

1 cup garlic cloves

1½ cups vegetable oil

1 (8-oz) jar Castelvetrano olives, pitted and halved

1 cup sliced Peppadew peppers

½ cup sliced pepperoncini peppers

Sprig of rosemary, leaves only, finely chopped

½ cup balsamic vinegar

6 Tbsp Garlic Oil (see here)

Arugula (optional)

1 log goat cheese

Red chili flakes, to taste

Pepper and flaky finishing salt, to taste

Crackers or bread, to serve

Olive Appetizer

SERVES
10–12

This appetizer was designed to replace a stuffed-olive dish that had been on the menu. You can marinate the olives and roast the garlic days in advance and have them ready to serve with your favorite log of goat cheese and crackers. Take this snack to your next potluck or beach day.

Garlic oil Preheat oven to 325°F.

Place garlic in a small baking dish. Cover with enough oil to fully submerge the garlic. Cover with aluminum foil and bake for 15 to 20 minutes, until garlic is lightly browned and softened. Drain the garlic oil into a jar and save for another use, reserving roasted garlic. Garlic oil will keep refrigerated in an airtight container for up to 2 weeks.

Olives and peppers In a bowl, combine olives, sliced peppers, and rosemary. Stir in balsamic vinegar and garlic oil.

Assembly To serve, place arugula (if using) on a serving platter. Softly break up the log of goat cheese and top with olives, peppers, and roasted garlic. Season with chili flakes, pepper, and finishing salt. Serve with your favorite crackers or bread for scooping up.

PIZZA DOUGH

½ tsp kosher salt

1 (¼-oz) package dry yeast

1 Tbsp extra-virgin olive oil, plus extra for greasing

5½ cups "00" flour, plus extra for dusting

WALNUT PESTO

¼ cup walnuts

1 clove garlic, roughly chopped

¼ cup fresh parsley

¼ cup grated Parmigiano-Reggiano

1 cup extra-virgin olive oil

½ cup loosely packed fresh basil leaves

Salt, to taste

WHIPPED FETA

½ cup feta crumbles

½ cup whole milk

Grated zest of ¼ lemon

2 Tbsp heavy cream

2 tsp extra-virgin olive oil

Salt and pepper, to taste

ASSEMBLY

2 oz sun-dried tomatoes

3 oz artichoke hearts

3 oz pre-cooked shredded chicken of your choice

Privateer Pizza

MAKES
3
(12-inch) pizzas

The Privateer Pizza is one of Privateer's most popular pizzas. "It's one of our most unique and flavorful," says chef Oscar Garcia. If you're using a coal-fired or wood-fired oven, crank it up to 800°F to achieve the ideal blistered crust.

Pizza dough In the bowl of a stand mixer fitted with the hook attachment, combine 1½ cups of warm water, salt, yeast, and oil. Add flour and mix on low speed for 9 minutes. The dough should be tacky but not sticky. Place dough into a large oiled container with a tight-fitting lid. Cover and set aside to rise at room temperature for about 2 hours. Divide into 3 portions, form into balls, and place each into an oiled container. Cover and set aside at room temperature until ready to use.

Walnut pesto Combine walnuts, garlic, parsley, and Parmigiano-Reggiano in a food processor and blend until smooth. Add oil and basil in parts, alternating adding the ingredients, and blend until the mixture is emulsified and smooth, about 2 minutes. Season to taste with salt.

Whipped feta Combine feta, milk, and lemon zest in a food processor and blend for 3 minutes.

While the processor is running, add cream and drizzle in oil until the feta is smooth, about 3 minutes more. Season to taste with salt and pepper.

Assembly Preheat the oven to 500°F, or 800°F if using a wood/coal-fired oven.

Using the tips of your fingers, flatten one dough ball on a clean surface. Using the palms of your hands, stretch it into a 12-inch disk. To help, you can pick up the dough by the "crust" and let gravity stretch it out, rotating along the edge until it's 12 inches wide. Repeat for the other dough balls.

If using a wood/coal-fired oven, place dough on a well-floured paddle (or if using a conventional oven, on a baking sheet that is lightly floured or lined with parchment paper). Stretch the dough to the edges of the paddle or baking sheet. Top prepared pizza rounds with the pesto and whipped feta, equally divided, then add tomatoes, artichokes, and chicken.

Bake for 12 to 15 minutes in a conventional oven, or for 4 to 6 minutes in a wood/coal-fired oven, until the crust blisters. Serve immediately.

RANCH 45

▶ *SOLANA BEACH* ◀

CHEF / DuVal Warner

RANCH 45, located on the Solana Beach and Del Mar border, is many things: a casual, outdoor restaurant for breakfast burritos, burgers for lunch, and steaks for dinner; and also a butchery, and a retail shop for wine, coffee, and more. For chef DuVal Warner, a U.S. Marine Corps veteran who began culinary school just shy of two weeks after retiring from the military, it's a place for fellowship. He credits his service for preparing him well for the restaurant industry. "It's still a chain of command, and the mission for me as a chef in a restaurant is to provide great service, great food, for great people," Warner says.

The food focuses on comforting American classics highlighting the region's farms and purveyors. Breakfast items feature eggs from Eben-Haezer Egg Ranch in Ramona, and plant-paired dishes are centered around whatever's growing at Chino Farm in Rancho Santa Fe. The steak tasting is equal parts full meal and sampling of prime Brandt Beef cuts guests can take home from the butcher case.

Ranch 45 is also known for customizing orders specific to guests' needs. They've provided bones for the bone broth for a customer whose parents are going through cancer treatment and recovery, and sold beef organs to dog owners who feed their pets a raw diet. The extra bit of flexibility and care Ranch 45 offers isn't often found at the typical grocery store. "Food is family," Warner says. "Being able to provide food for friends or family and knowing that people are taken care of, knowing that they can enjoy a good meal, something that you prepared, that's satisfying to me."

▶ *Brandt Beef Steak Tasting with Wedge Salad*

CHIMICHURRI

½ jalapeño, seeded and finely diced

½ cup finely diced white onion

1 clove garlic

1 tsp kosher salt

¼ tsp red chili flakes

1 Tbsp red wine vinegar

½ cup extra-virgin olive oil

1 bunch cilantro, finely chopped

1 bunch parsley, finely chopped

2 Tbsp oregano leaves

STEAK SAUCE

1 (17-oz) package Brandt Beef Demi-Glace (see Note)

1 sprig fresh thyme

¼ cup (½ stick) unsalted butter, diced

Salt and pepper, to taste

STEAK

1 (4-oz) Brandt Beef Prime Tenderloin (see Note)

1 (4-oz) Brandt Beef Prime Ribeye (see Note)

Salt and pepper, to taste

¾ cup (1½ sticks) unsalted butter, diced

1 sprig fresh rosemary, leaves only

1 sprig fresh thyme, leaves only

French fries, to serve

Brandt Beef Steak Tasting with Wedge Salad

SERVES
1–2

This steak recipe features a basting method that creates a deep brown crust. You'll need a food thermometer, but if you don't have one, try the hand test. To check for doneness, chef DuVal Warner says, "Compare the feeling of the cooked meat to the flesh on your hand. A rare steak will be soft, like the flesh on an open hand. A well-done steak is firm, like the flesh when you press your pinky finger to your thumb."

Chimichurri (see Note) Combine all ingredients in a large mixing bowl, adding your herbs last. Mix well and set aside.

NOTE *Chimichurri can also be made in a blender or food processor. To do so, add all ingredients and blend in small batches to ensure herbs incorporate evenly but are not puréed.*

Steak sauce In a small saucepan over medium-high heat, combine the demi-glace and thyme, stirring occasionally to prevent browning the bottom of the pan, and bring to a boil. Reduce heat to medium-low and simmer for 20 minutes. Remove from heat, add butter, and stir. Season to taste with salt and pepper. Keep warm.

NOTE *Brandt Beef Demi-Glace may be purchased at Ranch 45 or online.*

WEDGE SALAD

1 head iceberg lettuce

1 (12-oz) package Brandt Beef All
Natural Beef Bacon, cut into small
strips or cubes (see Note)

1 (12-oz) package of cherry tomatoes,
quartered

Salt and pepper, to taste

Zest and juice of 1 lemon, to taste

¼ cup blue cheese dressing

¼ cup blue cheese crumbles

½ cup crushed croutons

Steak Set steaks on the counter for at least 25 minutes to bring to room temperature. Season steaks with salt and pepper. Heat a cast-iron pan on high heat for a few minutes. Add butter and wait until melted and amber in color, then add steaks to pan. Sear for 7 to 8 minutes, tilting the pan and basting each steak with butter, until a deep brown crust forms. Flip steaks and repeat until they reach an internal temperature of 130°F for medium doneness. (While resting, steak temperature will rise another 8 to 10 degrees.) Season with salt and pepper to taste and garnish with herbs. Serve with fries, chimichurri, and steak sauce.

NOTE Brandt Beef Prime Tenderloin, Prime Ribeye, and All Natural Beef Bacon may be purchased at Ranch 45 or online.

Wedge salad Clean iceberg lettuce of any loose leaves. Cut in half, then cut the two halves in half to make your wedges. (If you prefer, you can stretch one head of lettuce from 4 wedges to 16 mini wedges to make a salad platter for an appetizer salad.)

In a pan on medium to high heat, cook bacon for 8 to 10 minutes until crispy, or until your desired doneness. Transfer bacon to a paper towel–lined plate to drain. (Reserve bacon fat for another use.) In a bowl, season tomatoes with salt, pepper, and lemon zest and juice, to taste. To serve, place lettuce wedges on plates and dress with seasoned tomatoes, blue cheese dressing, and blue cheese crumbles. Top with crushed croutons and bacon. Season to taste with salt and pepper.

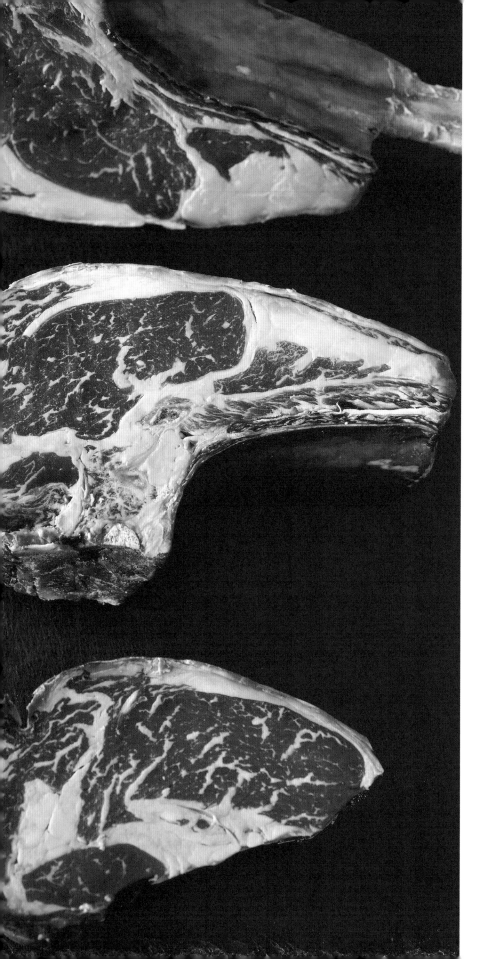

1 (2-lb) Brandt Beef shoulder or chuck roast, cut into ½-inch cubes

½ tsp kosher salt

¼ tsp pepper

¼ cup olive oil

1 white onion, finely chopped

3 stalks celery, finely chopped

⅓ cup chopped baby carrots, in ⅓-inch pieces

3 cloves garlic, minced

2 cups sliced fingerling potatoes

1 Tbsp tomato paste

½ tsp red chili flakes

½ cup red wine

1½ qts bone broth

Sprig of thyme

Chopped Italian parsley, for garnish

Chopped chives, for garnish

1 loaf sourdough, sliced and grilled

Braised Brandt Beef Stew

Chef DuVal Warner suggests using a red wine of your choice but to avoid anything that's overly sweet. Prepare the stew a day in advance, which will allow the flavors to meld.

Stew Season beef with salt and pepper.

Heat oil in a Dutch oven over medium-high heat. Add beef and sear for 5 minutes, until browned all over. Reduce heat to medium. Add onion and sauté for 3 minutes, until translucent. Add celery and carrots and sauté for another 2 minutes. Stir in garlic, potatoes, tomato paste, and chili flakes.

Pour in wine and cook for 4 to 5 minutes, until reduced by half. Add broth and thyme. Bring to a boil. Cover, then reduce heat to medium-low and simmer for 1 hour, until beef is fork tender. Remove thyme.

To serve, ladle stew into bowls and sprinkle with parsley and chives. Serve with grilled sourdough.

SAKI SAKI SUSHI BAR & GRILL

▶ *CARMEL MOUNTAIN* ◀

CHEF / Shant Ohanian

SAKI SAKI is an anomaly among a sea of national chain eateries in Carmel Mountain, a suburb in North County. When Los Angeles native Shant Ohanian took over the restaurant located in a sprawling shopping center in 2022, he brought his personal experiences with him, from cooking in Italian kitchens to making weekly taco trips to Tijuana. He also insisted on fresh, local ingredients where possible. These experiences are reflected in Saki Saki's eclectic sushi rolls—which, despite all the accoutrements, like the Diablo roll's ponzu sauce and Sriracha drizzle, still allow the quality of the fish to shine. Ohanian's Asian spin on carbonara features pan-fried char siu and miso, while Hokkaido scallops are the star of his aguachile.

After culinary school, Ohanian cut his teeth in restaurants in Los Angeles, including the now-defunct Ketchup. Yet entrepreneurship and the less congested roads of San Diego would lead him to Saki Saki. When his Armenian parents immigrated from Iran, his dad bought a pizza-delivery franchise and expanded the business to forty locations. "I quite literally grew up in them," Ohanian says. He would go on to open a few franchises of his own before moving to San Diego. And though he took a break from hospitality, the industry kept reeling him back. He finds fulfillment in making people happy through food and interacting with guests who end up becoming friends. Plus, "You never know who's gonna walk through the door," Ohanian says.

3 cups heavy cream

1 cup sugar

¼ cup store-bought yuzu juice
(see Note)

1 tsp vanilla extract

Confectioners' sugar, for dusting

6 mint leaves, for garnish

No-Bake Yuzu Custard

"This delicious dessert blends French and Japanese flavors," explains Shant Ohanian. "Tart yuzu juice and the sweetness from sugar and vanilla is a perfect combination—not too sweet, not too sour. Plus, the aroma is delightful."

Custard Combine cream and sugar in a saucepan and gently simmer over medium heat for 3 minutes, until sugar has dissolved. Remove from heat, then stir in yuzu juice and vanilla. Pour mixture into six (4-ounce) ramekins, then refrigerate for at least 2 hours, but preferably overnight.

To serve, dust custard with confectioners' sugar and garnish with mint.

NOTE *Yuzu is a sweet and zingy Japanese citrus fruit with a grapefruit-orange flavor. Find the juice at Asian food shops or fine food specialists. Alternatively, use an equal amount of fresh lemon juice.*

MISO BUTTER

½ cup (1 stick) salted butter

2 Tbsp white miso

PASTA

4 cups rotini pasta

CHEESE SAUCE

1 cup grated mild cheddar

1 cup grated Monterey Jack

½ cup Miso Butter (see here)

1½ cups heavy cream

1 tsp MSG (optional)

1 tsp pepper

Crispy fried onions, for garnish (see Note)

Bunch of chives, finely chopped, for garnish

Miso Mac and Cheese

"For this twist on an American classic, prepare the miso butter a day ahead so it can meld in the refrigerator overnight," says Shant Ohanian. "Or, in a pinch, refrigerate for at least 2 hours."

Miso butter In a small bowl, combine butter and miso and mix until well incorporated. Refrigerate, preferably overnight.

Pasta Bring a medium saucepan of salted water to a boil. Add pasta and cook according to package instructions, until al dente. Drain, then rinse under cold running water. Set aside.

Cheese sauce Combine grated cheeses in a bowl.

In a large saucepan, melt the miso butter, then add cream and three-quarters of the cheese blend. Heat over medium heat until cheese has melted and the sauce comes together. Stir in pasta, MSG (if using), and pepper.

Transfer to a serving dish and garnish with crispy onions, chives, and remaining cheese.

NOTE Crispy fried onions can be found at Asian markets and in the fresh salad sections of many grocery stores.

SMOKIN J'S BBQ

▶ *GASLAMP, MIRAMAR, POWAY* ◀

OWNERS / Jeremy George
and Josh George

FARMERS' MARKET regulars may be familiar with Smokin J's BBQ, who began slinging its unique mash-up of Kansas City– and Texas-inspired smoked meats across the county in 2016. From their pop-up success, brothers Josh and Jeremy George, and Jeremy's wife Mckenzie, opened the first Smokin J's brick-and-mortar location in Old Town Poway—later supplying its hours-long-fire-whispered proteins to the Miramar and Gaslamp locations.

"We've sprung from traditional Texas-style [BBQ], and Jeremy's designed a range of rubs that are more than salt and pepper," Josh says. The Smokin J's house sauce borrows from Kansas City BBQ sauce, but is less sweet. Its eponymous Smokin J brisket with pork belly sandwich is a favorite, and comes together over five days. Pork belly is first cured, then smoked for four hours. "Then we're braising it for another four hours in pork stock, chilling it down, frying it, and slicing it to order," Jeremy says. The brisket smokes for around sixteen hours.

Lured by the warm weather and, at the time, lack of BBQ options in San Diego, Jeremy and Mckenzie ditched careers in finance in Virginia, where the George brothers grew up, to bring more BBQ to San Diego. Josh, a former professional athlete and member of the U.S. Paralympic track and field team, followed Jeremy to San Diego shortly after to help grow the business. And while Smokin J's blends barbeque styles from different corners of the country, they've also keyed in on San Diegans' love language—tacos and burritos, Smokin J's style. That is, stuffed with brisket that's been smoked low and slow.

BREAD PUDDING

2 lbs stale brioche, cut into 1-inch cubes

2 cups milk

1 cup heavy cream

½ cup sugar

1½ tsp vanilla extract

1 Tbsp ground cinnamon

1½ tsp ground nutmeg

½ tsp salt

8 large eggs

2 Tbsp brisket fat, lard, or butter, for greasing

¼ cup turbinado sugar

CARAMEL SAUCE

¼ cup (½ stick) butter

½ cup light corn syrup (preferably Karo)

1½ cups packed brown sugar

½ cup heavy cream

ASSEMBLY

⅓ cup (⅔ stick) butter

Bread Pudding with Caramel Drizzle

SERVES
6

This recipe features brioche and warming spices like cinnamon and nutmeg.

Bread pudding Put brioche cubes in a large bowl.

In a large saucepan, combine milk, cream, sugar, vanilla, cinnamon, nutmeg, and salt. Heat over medium heat, stirring occasionally, until the temperature reaches 125°F.

Meanwhile, whisk eggs in a large bowl. Ladle ½ cup of the hot mixture into the eggs, stirring with a whisk. Do not whisk too hard as it will add air to the eggs. Gradually add the remaining hot mixture, 1 cup at a time, and stir.

Pour batter over the brioche. When cool enough to handle, use your hands to mix until bread cubes are coated. Set aside for 1 hour.

Preheat oven to 300°F. Grease a 10- × 12-inch baking pan with fat (or butter) and lightly coat with turbinado sugar. Transfer the battered brioche into the pan and bake, uncovered, for 1 hour, until the top is golden brown but the bread is still moist. Set aside to cool slightly.

Cut into squares and keep warm.

Caramel sauce Heat butter and corn syrup in a small saucepan over medium heat, until butter has melted. Add brown sugar and bring to a simmer. Simmer for 4 minutes, until sauce is smooth. Remove from heat, then stir in cream.

Assembly Melt butter in a skillet over medium-low heat. Fry each side of the bread pudding squares, until dark golden brown. Transfer to plates, then drizzle caramel sauce overtop with a spoon.

Ingredients

SMOKED BRISKET CHILI

¼ cup oil (any kind) or brisket fat

1 yellow onion, coarsely chopped

1 large red bell pepper, seeded, deveined, and chopped

¾ cup tomato paste

2 tomatoes, chopped (2 cups)

1½ cups beef stock

1 (12-oz) can dark lager

1 Tbsp ground cumin

2 tsp kosher salt

2 tsp chili powder

1 tsp cayenne pepper

1 tsp cumin seeds

1 tsp dried oregano

1 tsp cocoa powder

2 qts chopped Smokin J's smoked brisket

Aged white cheddar, for topping

Chopped red onion, for topping

CORNBREAD

2 cups all-purpose flour

2 cups yellow cornmeal

1 cup sugar

2 Tbsp baking powder

1 tsp salt

4 large eggs

1 qt buttermilk

1⅛ cups (2¼ sticks) butter (divided)

1 cup frozen corn

HONEY-BUTTER GLAZE

½ cup (1 stick) butter

½ cup honey (divided)

Smoked Brisket Chili with Cornbread

"This quick-cook chili is a great way to repurpose leftover smoked brisket or steak," says Jeremy. "Serve with a fluffy piece of fresh-baked cornbread crumbled over your chili or on the side with a bit of butter."

Smoked brisket chili Heat oil (or fat) in a stockpot over medium heat. Add onion and bell pepper and sauté for 3 minutes. Stir in tomato paste and cook for another 3 minutes, taking care not to burn. Reduce heat if needed.

Stir in tomatoes, stock, and lager. Add spices and cocoa powder, then bring to a simmer. Add brisket and simmer, uncovered, for 45 minutes to 1 hour, until thickened to your desired consistency.

Cornbread Preheat oven to 350°F. Place a 10- × 12-inch baking pan in the oven.

In a large bowl, combine flour, cornmeal, sugar, baking powder, and salt. Mix well, breaking up any clumps.

In a separate bowl, whisk eggs and buttermilk. Using a rubber spatula, stir mixture into the dry ingredients.

Melt 1 cup (2 sticks) butter in a small saucepan over medium-low heat. Stir melted butter into the batter, working quickly to incorporate butter before it hardens. Stir in corn.

Remove the hot pan from the oven and grease the bottom and sides with the remaining ⅛ cup (¼ stick) of butter. Pour batter into the hot pan and bake for 30 minutes, until the surface begins to harden.

Honey-butter glaze Meanwhile, melt butter in a small saucepan over medium heat. Skim the milk solids from the surface to clarify butter. (While the milk solids do not impact the taste, they can look unappealing on top of your cornbread.) Whisk in ¼ cup honey and set aside for 30 minutes.

Assembly Once cornbread has just started to firm up, brush with honey-butter glaze. Drizzle the remaining ¼ cup of honey on top and bake for another 15 to 20 minutes, until golden and a toothpick inserted into the center comes out clean.

Spoon chili into bowls and top with cheddar and red onion. Serve with cornbread.

SPLIT BAKEHOUSE

▶ *LA MESA* ◀

CHEF / Vanessa Corrales

"WE EAT with our eyes," Vanessa Corrales, founder of Split Bakehouse in La Mesa, says. As a café manager in 2015, Corrales noted how difficult it was to source vegan baked goods, and that most of what was available looked drab and unappealing. Her colorful vegan pastries, from scones to pop tarts, are anything but. Her path to a thriving bakery was also colorful. She often sports rainbow-colored hair, clothing, and accessories herself!

The success of her certified-organic cotton candy business prior to Split supported the bakery's fledgling years. Corrales remembers working around the clock to glaze, package, and deliver pastries, catching a few winks in her car, then heading back to the bakery to rinse and repeat. "Failure was not an option," Corrales says. As a born-and-raised San Diegan, she watched her entrepreneurial family begin several businesses and internalized the fact that challenges often meant finding another door to walk through. She learned to lean into possibility as part of her hospitality training when she helped open the Fairmont Grand Del Mar.

Corrales hopes to expand beyond Split's pre-order window and kitchen to offer even fancier vegan baked goods and desserts in a café setting, and to continue sending the bakery's employees abroad—from Spain to France to Mexico. Corrales looks forward to the creativity her team brings back to Split's baked goods. "They don't have to taste like cardboard," Corrales says of plant-based treats.

½ cup raw cashews

1 cup filtered water

¾ tsp salt

1 Tbsp potato flour

⅓ cup sunflower lecithin

3 Tbsp refined coconut oil

¼ cup canned pickled jalapeños, chopped

Vegan Jalapeño Cream Cheese

Instead of jalapeños, you can add fruit or roasted garlic or fresh chopped herbs to this savory spread.

Cream cheese Place cashews in a bowl and add enough tap water to cover. Soak for at least 12 hours or overnight in the refrigerator.

Drain cashews, then place them in a blender. Add filtered water and salt and blend on high speed for 2 minutes. Add potato flour and sunflower lecithin and blend for another minute. With the motor running, slowly pour in coconut oil and blend for 2 minutes, until smooth. Add pickled jalapeños to the blender and pulse a few times, until incorporated.

Vegan jalapeño cream cheese can be stored in an airtight container in the refrigerator for up to 7 days.

EGG SUBSTITUTE

2 cups golden flax meal

1 cup oat milk

1 cup apple sauce

2 ripe bananas

MUFFINS

Nonstick cooking spray

5 cups all-purpose or whole-wheat flour

4 tsp baking soda

1 Tbsp baking powder

1 tsp salt

9 bananas

1½ cups piloncillo sugar

1 cup + 2 Tbsp avocado oil

⅓ cup Egg Substitute (see here)

1 Tbsp vanilla extract

⅓ cup vegan chocolate chips (see Note)

Vegan Piloncillo, Banana, and Chocolate Chip Muffins

MAKES

12 muffins

These muffins combine rich piloncillo sugar and ripe bananas with chocolate chips for some textural crunch. They're ideal as an easy snack or a cozy breakfast treat. "Transform basic ingredients into a batch of heavenly goodness in just thirty minutes," says Vanessa Corrales.

The egg substitute makes a great vegan binder and can be used as an egg substitute for most baking recipes.

Egg substitute In a blender, combine flax meal and oat milk and blend for a minute. Add the apple sauce and bananas and blend for another minute, until smooth.

Leftover egg substitute can be stored in an airtight container in the refrigerator for up to 3 weeks.

Muffins Preheat oven to 350°F. Spray a twelve-cup muffin tin with nonstick cooking spray or line with cupcake liners.

In a medium bowl, whisk together flour, baking soda, baking powder, and salt.

In a food processor or blender, combine bananas, piloncillo sugar, avocado oil, egg substitute, and vanilla. Mix on medium-low for 30 to 45 seconds, until combined and slightly chunky. Add wet ingredients to dry ingredients and mix. Fold in chocolate chips.

Fill muffin cups three-quarters full. Bake for 20 to 25 minutes, until a toothpick inserted into the center comes out clean. Cool on a wire rack.

NOTE *The chocolate chips can be replaced with walnuts, peanut butter chips, dried fruit, raisins, cranberries, or shredded coconut. Have fun with the variations!*

TAHONA

▶ *OLD TOWN* ◀

CHEF / Adrian Villarreal

"**EVERY TIME** I lose north, I always come back to mezcal," say Adrian Villarreal, executive chef and partner at Tahona. The agave-based spirit is Tahona's culinary anchor. It guides the food menu. At Tahona, "Food is the rhythm guitar and mezcal is the lead singer," he says, drawing on his music background. Then adds, "We cater the food to the mezcal experience." Tahona's commitment to mezcal research and education is a huge reason why Villarreal was drawn to the concept, which opened in Old Town in 2018.

Its menu begins in Oaxaca, the land of *mole*, and traverses Baja and southern California. Villarreal grew up in Tijuana and crossed the border to San Diego regularly. His culinary perspective is just as diverse, informed by time spent working for top chefs in Baja, in Peru, and at Noma in Copenhagen. For example, his use of a wok, a technique Villarreal picked up in Peru that imparts a smoky flavor to dishes, is typically frowned upon in the context of his French culinary training. At Tahona, Villarreal employs the technique to season dishes.

There are fish plates, tostadas, and *antojitos* (Mexican street food), like tempura squash blossoms with eggplant crema and a carnitas bao bun with pistachio macha. The use of ash and dark plates acknowledges Tahona's location next to a cemetery. One might notice the theme in its poached and charred octopus dish. "It's the kitchen's favorite protein to play with," Villarreal says.

▶ *Rabbit Adobado Taco with Pineapple Pico and Charred Avocado and Tempura Squash Blossom with Charred Eggplant Emulsion, Herb Vinaigrette, and Smoked Cheese*

CHARRED EGGPLANT EMULSION

1 eggplant

1 cup extra-virgin olive oil (divided)

½ cup rice wine vinegar

Salt and pepper, to taste

HERB VINAIGRETTE

2 cloves garlic confit or 2 Tbsp garlic purée

Bunch of parsley, chopped

¼ bunch mint, chopped

¼ bunch basil, chopped

¼ bunch chives, chopped

2 cups extra-virgin olive oil

1 cup lemon juice

Salt and pepper, to taste

TEMPURA SQUASH BLOSSOM

2 qts vegetable oil, for frying

1 cup heirloom corn masa (see Note)

1 organic egg

Pinch of oregano

Salt and pepper, to taste

12 squash blossoms with baby zucchini attached (see Note)

ASSEMBLY

Pea tendrils, for garnish

Olive oil, for drizzling

Fresh squash blossom leaves, for garnish

Sorrel, for garnish

Smoked aged sheep's milk cheese (preferably Idiazábal)

Lime wedges, to serve

Tempura Squash Blossom with Charred Eggplant Emulsion, Herb Vinaigrette, and Smoked Cheese

MAKES
12
blossoms

Charred eggplant emulsion Preheat a grill over high heat. Add eggplant and grill for 15 minutes, until charred on all sides. Set aside to cool, then roughly chop.

In a blender, combine eggplant, ½ cup oil, and vinegar and blend. With the blender running, slowly pour in the remaining ½ cup oil, until creamy and glossy. If needed, thin out with a little water. Season to taste with salt and pepper. Keep warm.

Herb vinaigrette Combine all ingredients in a food processor. Blend until emulsified. Season to taste with salt and pepper. Set aside.

Tempura squash blossom Heat oil in a deep fryer or deep saucepan to a temperature of 350°F.

In a blender, combine masa, egg, oregano, salt, and pepper. Add 6 tablespoons of water and blend until it has the consistency of light cream.

Using clean tweezers, remove stamens from squash blossoms and discard. Gently wipe the flowers clean. Dip blossoms in the batter horizontally to coat. Carefully lower blossoms into oil and deep-fry for 3 to 4 minutes, rotating until evenly fried. Transfer to a paper towel–lined plate to drain. Season with salt and pepper.

NOTE In Mexican cooking, masa is the traditional, corn-based flour used to make tortillas, tamales, and more.

Assembly Spread eggplant emulsion on the plates. Arrange squash blossoms on top and drizzle with vinaigrette.

In a small bowl, toss pea tendrils in a drizzle of oil. Garnish the plates with the pea tendrils, fresh squash blossom leaves, sorrel, and finely grated cheese. Serve with lime wedges.

NOTE Squash blossoms can be purchased seasonally at farmers' or Mexican markets. Male squash blossoms are an acceptable alternative but won't have the baby zucchini attached.

RABBIT TERRINE

1 lb ground chicken

1 lb ground rabbit

2 Tbsp kosher salt

1 Tbsp garlic powder

1 Tbsp pepper

2 tsp transglutaminase (see Note)

Pinch of oregano

PINEAPPLE PICO

1 (1-lb) organic pineapple, peeled and cored

5 shallots, finely chopped

4 scallions, thinly sliced

2 habanero peppers, cleaned, deveined, and finely chopped

¼ cup key lime juice

2 Tbsp extra-virgin olive oil

Salt and pepper, to taste

ADOBO

1 cup tomato purée

1 cup pineapple juice

¼ cup achiote paste, plus extra to taste

Dash of white vinegar

Salt and pepper, to taste

Rabbit Adobado Taco with Pineapple Pico and Charred Avocado

SERVES

6

Rabbit terrine Combine all ingredients in a large bowl and mix well. Fry a small piece of the mixture in a skillet until cooked through. Taste and adjust seasoning, if necessary.

Transfer mixture to a 9- × 13-inch baking pan. Set aside for 30 minutes.

Preheat oven to 325°F. Cover pan with aluminum foil and bake for 45 minutes, until meat reaches a temperature of 165°F. Set aside to rest for 15 minutes. Transfer to a cutting board. Cut into 2-ounce slices.

Pineapple pico Preheat a grill over high heat. Add pineapple and grill for 3 minutes per side, until slightly charred all around. Transfer pineapple to a cutting board and chop into ¼-inch cubes.

In a bowl, combine pineapple and remaining ingredients and mix well. Season to taste with salt and pepper.

Adobo Combine all ingredients in a blender and blend until smooth. Season to taste with more achiote paste.

NOTE Transglutaminase is a naturally occurring enzyme used in the culinary world to bind proteins. It is typically sold in powder form and can be purchased online.

ASSEMBLY

2 avocados, peeled and pitted

12 (6-inch) heirloom corn tortillas
(see Note)

Cilantro sprouts, for garnish

Assembly Preheat a grill over high heat. Cut
each avocado half into 4 slices. Add to grill and
char each side. Remove from grill and set aside.

Heat tortillas in a skillet over medium-low heat,
then keep warm.

Using the same skillet over medium-high heat,
warm slices of rabbit terrine and generously
brush with adobo.

Plate 2 tortillas per serving, then top with rabbit
terrine. Garnish with pico, charred avocado, and
cilantro sprouts. Serve immediately.

NOTE *Heirloom corn often refers to native or
cultivated varieties that have been passed down
generations and planted by smaller farms, as
opposed to industrially produced varieties. Find
heirloom corn tortillas at specialty grocers, such
as Whole Foods, or online.*

TANNER'S PRIME BURGERS

▶ *DEL MAR, OCEANSIDE* ◀

CHEF / Brandon Rodgers

TANNER'S PRIME BURGERS in Oceanside and at the Del Mar Thoroughbred Club demonstrates there's more to cooking up the perfect smash burger than slapping meat on the griddle. It all starts with 100% USDA Prime all-natural beef. Tanner's sources their beef from Brandt Beef, a multi-generational southern California family operation since 1945. Then you need to hold the seasoning, and give the patty room to breathe. "If you season the beef before it goes down [on the griddle] the salt is going to pull out the moisture of the beef," Rodgers explains. Meaning lackluster caramelization, if it happens at all. Instead, smash unseasoned beef evenly with uneven edges, so it creates air pockets for the steam to escape through. "Little volcanoes, as I call them," Rodgers says. Otherwise, the patty won't crisp.

As a young chef, Rodgers dove into the fine dining world after graduating from the New England Culinary Institute, including The French Laundry in Napa, Daniel in NYC, and as chef de cuisine of three-Michelin-starred Benu in San Francisco. He was selected as sous chef to represent the U.S. in the prestigious Bocuse d'Or competition in France, and was twice nominated for the Best Chef: California category of the James Beard Awards.

Rodgers sees creative parallels between fine dining and the fast-casual format of Tanner's. Rather than serving fifty people a night, Rodgers says, the riddle becomes how to serve a premium product out of something so common as a burger, and one that's accessible to the masses? "There's enjoyment and a challenge in being able to accomplish that."

▶ *Tanner's Prime Double Burger and Tanner's Prime Hot Sauce*

CARAMELIZED BEEF BACON AND ONIONS

1 (12-oz) package Brandt Beef All Natural Beef Bacon, cut into ¼-inch pieces

2 jumbo sweet yellow onions, cut into ¼-inch dice

BURGER

Tanner's Beef Tallow, for greasing

4 lbs Brandt Beef all-natural ground beef

Salt and pepper, to taste

12 slices American cheese (preferably New School)

6 brioche buns, toasted

Tanner's Prime Burger Sauce

6 leaves iceberg lettuce

½ yellow onion, thinly sliced

2 vine-ripened tomatoes, thinly sliced

6 jarred cascabella peppers, to serve

Tanner's Prime Hot Sauce (page 161), to serve

Tanner's Prime Double Burger

SERVES
6

"Tanner's burger starts with Brandt Beef: single-sourced from one family, one ranch, and one breed out of Brawley," says chef Brandon Rodgers. He then adds, "We smash our burgers thin for maximum caramelization. The meat separates from itself and has visible air pockets, which is good since it allows the moisture to escape and creates caramelization and a crispy sear!"

Brandt Beef products can be purchased online, while the beef tallow and burger sauce can be purchased at Tanner's.

Caramelized beef bacon and onions In a skillet over medium heat, render bacon for 6 to 8 minutes, until slightly crispy. Transfer bacon to a paper towel–lined plate. Reserve fat in pan.

Add onions to the skillet and cook for about 25 minutes, stirring frequently, until evenly caramelized. Drain fat, mix in bacon, and set aside.

Burger Preheat griddle to 400°F. Lightly grease the griddle with beef tallow.

Divide beef into 12 equal portions and shape into patties. (We do not season before we sear because the salt draws out moisture from the meat, which combats the caramelization and crispy sear.) Place patties onto the hot griddle and, using a burger press, press firmly in a circular motion to a ¼-inch thickness.

Season patties with salt and pepper evenly across the surface. Using a putty knife or bench scraper, scrape under the patty for a clean release of beef. This is critical as you want the crust to remain intact, not stick to the griddle.

Flip patties. Working fast, add a large spoonful of caramelized beef bacon and onions and a slice of cheese to each patty and cook until cheese melts. Remove from the griddle.

To build the burgers, place each brioche bun bottom on a 12- × 12-inch sheet of parchment-lined foil. Top with burger sauce, lettuce, onion slices, and tomato. Add 2 patties, more burger sauce, and the brioche bun top. Fold and wrap foil around burger, to keep all ingredients together and make it easy to eat.

Serve with cascabella peppers and hot sauce.

FERMENTED MASH

2 oz dried chiles de arbol, stemmed

2 oz dried guajillo chiles, stemmed

1 lb red bell peppers, stemmed and quartered

1½ cups distilled water

¼ cup kosher salt

SAUCE

Fermented Mash (see here)

4 cups distilled vinegar

3 cups distilled water

Tanner's Prime Hot Sauce

MAKES about 75 ounces or 15 (5-ounce) bottles

This small-batch hot sauce was specifically created to spice up the menu items at Tanner's. "It's crafted to erupt a burst of flavor in every bite. Don't be shy—douse it on and get saucy!" says chef Brandon Rodgers.

You'll need a high-powered blender, a fermentation bucket, and a pH meter. Alternatively, you can purchase Tanner's Prime Hot Sauce at Tanner's.

Fermented mash Bring 2 cups of water to a simmer in a saucepan. Place dried chiles in a bowl and add enough hot water to cover. Set aside for 1 hour. Drain, then place into a high-powered blender. Add bell peppers, distilled water, and salt and blend to a chunky mash.

Place mash in a fermentation bucket and store at room temperature in a dark location for 14 days or until the pH is 3.9. If higher than that, ferment for a couple more days.

Sauce Working in batches, combine all ingredients in a blender and blend until smooth. The pH should be 3.9. If it is higher, add more vinegar until the pH reads 3.9 or lower.

Sauce can be stored in an airtight container and refrigerated for up to 6 months. Use whenever your dishes need a kick, like on a steak and eggs breakfast.

TJ OYSTER BAR

▶ *BONITA, CHULA VISTA* ◀

CO-OWNER (C) Alicia Diaz
CO-OWNER (L) Monica Jazo
CO-OWNER (R) Yvan Jazo

FAMILY-RUN TJ OYSTER BAR in the county's southeastern region is a local favorite for fresh *mariscos* (seafood in Spanish) like they make in Baja California. For twenty years, they've been serving fish tacos, octopus tostadas, whole fish plates, and shareables like smoked tuna fries. "Simple yet delicious," says co-owner Monica Jazo. They also do regional specialties, such as the stingray taco, which isn't seen too often on San Diego taco shop menus. With the stingray prepared in a stewy broth with tomatoes and chiles, it's a riff on a traditional Mexican stew known as *caguamanta*.

Monica was a teenager when she reluctantly began helping her mom in the restaurant's original Bonita location. "My mom didn't want to leave me at home," she explains. The original location at 4246 Bonita Road is a sliver of a place with walk-up counter service, bar seating, and a few tables. They've since opened two other locations— including one in Chula Vista and a full-service restaurant and bar on Bonita near the original spot—which came with its own learning curve, like managing waitstaff and keeping a full bar. Through TJ Oyster Bar's growth, Monica recognized an opportunity to support her family, shape the guest experience, and expand the business. Monica and her mom, Alicia, manage the two Bonita locations, and her brother, Yvan, runs the Chula Vista outpost.

▶ *Baja Fish Tacos and Clamato Preparado*

FISH TACOS

2 cups all-purpose flour

1 Tbsp garlic salt

1 Tbsp dried Mexican oregano

1 Tbsp baking powder

1½ cups club soda

1 cup yellow mustard

4 cups vegetable oil, for frying

2 lbs skinless halibut or tilapia, cut into 4- × 1¼-inch strips

BAJA SAUCE

2 cups mayonnaise

¼ cup lime juice

ASSEMBLY

18 small (5-inch) corn tortillas

½ cabbage, thinly sliced

1 large tomato, finely chopped

2 limes, cut into wedges, to serve

Your favorite salsa, to serve

Baja Fish Tacos

SERVES
4–6

These fish tacos are best enjoyed with the Clamato Preparado on page 165.

Fish tacos In a large bowl, combine flour, garlic salt, oregano, and baking powder. Add club soda and mustard and whisk until combined. Set aside.

Heat oil in a deep fryer or a large saucepan over high heat, until the temperature reaches 350°F. Do not allow it to get too hot. Reduce the heat to medium-high. Using tongs, dip fish into batter and then carefully lower into the hot oil. Work in batches if necessary. Deep-fry for 4 to 6 minutes, turning, until golden. Transfer to a paper towel–lined plate to drain.

Baja sauce Combine mayonnaise, lime juice, and ¼ cup of water in a bowl and whisk well.

Assembly Meanwhile, heat a large skillet over medium heat. Add tortillas, one or two at a time, and warm both sides.

Place warm tortillas on plates. Add 1 or 2 pieces of fish to each. Top with cabbage, tomato, and Baja sauce.

Serve with lime wedges and your favorite salsa.

Juice of ½ lime, plus extra for rim

½ cup Tajín seasoning, for rim

½ cup Clamato juice

1 tsp Worcestershire sauce

Pinch of salt

Pinch of pepper

Tabasco, to taste

Ice

1 (12-oz) can or bottle of your favorite beer

Lime slice/wedge or celery stick, for garnish

Clamato Preparado

SERVES
1

Rim a mug or glass with lime. Place Tajín on a plate and rim glass with it.

Add lime juice and Clamato to glass. Add remaining ingredients, except beer and garnish, and mix. Pour in your beer. Garnish with a lime slice or wedge (or celery stick).

VALLE

▶ *OCEANSIDE* ◀

CHEF / Roberto Alcocer

ROBERTO ALCOCER was already an established chef and restaurateur in Mexico's Guadalupe Valley when he seized an opportunity to open Valle in 2021. As a seasonal tasting menu–only restaurant at Mission Pacific Beach Resort in Oceanside, its modern interpretation of Mexican regional cuisine highlights handmade velvety *moles*, slow-braised lamb birria, and so much more. The dining experience begins in its elegant, stoneware-filled dining room or on its oceanfront patio, meanders over a few hours across eight courses and an optional wine pairing, and concludes with a tour of the immaculate kitchen.

Valle earned a Michelin star in 2023—a first for Alcocer, and for the rapidly evolving city of Oceanside. The recognition is a dream come true for the chef, whose culinary ambition bloomed when he moved to France after high school. Alcocer grew up in Ensenada in the Mexican state of Baja California, near the Guadalupe Valley. There, smoke is the region's culinary ethos—and that tradition is apparent in Valle's dishes. Char takes center stage in the restaurant's onion tart (page 170), and grilled avocado imparts a mild anise flavor to the guacamole. Alcocer invokes the words of a colleague: "Smoke is an ingredient."

AGUACHILE DE CHAYOTE

½ white onion, coarsely chopped

½ serrano chile, plus extra if needed

½ bunch cilantro

¼ cup coconut water

Juice of 10 key limes

Salt, to taste

2 to 3 chayotes, thinly sliced with a mandoline

½ Persian cucumber, thinly sliced with a mandoline

AVOCADO MOUSSE

1 avocado, peeled and pitted

Juice of 1 lime

Salt, to taste

1½ Tbsp extra-virgin olive oil

COCONUT GELÉE

4 cups coconut milk

2½ Tbsp sugar

⅓ tsp salt

1 Tbsp agar agar

ASSEMBLY (SEE NOTE)

Amaranth petals

Oxalis

Juice of 1 finger lime

Sea beans

Oyster leaf

Thinly sliced serrano pepper

Micro cilantro

Extra-virgin olive oil, for drizzling

Fleur de sel, for sprinkling

Tostadas raspadas, to serve

Aguachile de Chayote

SERVES
3–4

Aguachile de chayote Combine all ingredients, except chayotes and cucumber, in a blender and mix until smooth. Season to taste with salt and/or more serrano. Pass through a fine-mesh sieve.

Add chayotes and cucumber to the aguachile and allow to marinate for 20 minutes.

Avocado mousse Meanwhile, in a blender, combine avocado, lime juice, salt, and 1½ tablespoons of water. Blend until smooth. With the blender running, slowly add oil and blend until emulsified.

Coconut gelée In a saucepan, combine coconut milk, sugar, and salt and bring to a simmer over medium heat, until sugar has dissolved. Whisk in agar agar, little by little, until smooth.

Pour into a baking dish, to about ½ inch deep. Set aside for 30 minutes, until set. Cut into 1-inch cubes.

Assembly To serve, spread out a base of avocado mousse on a plate. Arrange ribbons of marinated chayote and cucumber on top. Garnish with amaranth and oxalis. Sprinkle finger lime juice on top.

Arrange coconut gelée, sea beans, oyster leaf, serrano, and cilantro on the plate. Drizzle with oil and sprinkle with fleur de sel. Flavor all of the ingredients by pouring ¼ cup of aguachile on top—it's meant to be saucy! Serve with tostadas raspadas.

NOTE Many of the garnishes add textures and flavors to complement the dish. They are designed to be adjusted with the seasons and entirely optional. They can be purchased at Girl & Dug Farm or Chino Farm.

5 carrots

4 stalks celery

2 onions

½ cup grapeseed oil,
or any neutral oil

1 head of garlic,
halved widthwise

¼ cup tomato paste

1½ cups red wine

4¼ qts vegetable stock

4 sprigs thyme

Salt, to taste

ONION ASH

Scraps of 1 to 2 peeled onions

TART SHELLS

½ cup + 2 Tbsp all-purpose flour,
plus extra for dusting

3½ Tbsp butter

1 to 2 Tbsp Onion Ash (see here)

2 Tbsp fish stock

1 Tbsp fish sauce

1½ tsp squid ink

Onion Tart
(Tarta de Cebolla)

Vegetable demi Place carrots, celery, and onions in a large cast-iron skillet on high heat and char for 5 to 15 minutes with no oil, turning occasionally, blackening vegetables without caramelizing so they remain savory.

Heat oil in a stockpot over high heat. Add garlic, cut side down, and sear for 2 to 5 minutes, or until golden, and reserve. Add charred vegetables and tomato paste to the pot and cook for 15 to 25 minutes, until deeply caramelized and sticking to the pan. Pour in wine, reduce heat to medium-low, and gently simmer for 10 to 15 minutes, until liquid has reduced to a quarter.

Add stock, reserved garlic, and thyme and bring to a boil. Reduce heat to medium-low and gently simmer uncovered for 45 to 60 minutes, until sauce is thick, reduced, and concentrated enough to coat the back of a spoon. Strain, then season to taste with salt.

Onion ash Preheat oven to 500°F. Place onion scraps on a baking sheet and char completely, then blend in a blender or food processor until pulverized. Sift to remove big pieces.

Tart shells Preheat oven to 350°F.

In a food processor, combine flour, butter, and ash and pulse briefly until it resembles wet sand. Transfer mixture to a bowl. Add stock, fish sauce, and squid ink. Knead for 5 minutes, until dough forms a smooth ball. Allow to rest for 30 minutes.

Place dough on a work surface lightly dusted with flour. Roll out as thin as possible, then line four or five (3-inch) tart molds. Using a fork, poke small holes in the bases of the tart shells and freeze for 20 minutes. Remove from freezer, then bake for 15 minutes, until crispy.

CHARRED ONION

2 to 3 onions, sliced into
4 or 5 (1-inch) steaks
3½ Tbsp black vinegar
1½ Tbsp butter
Salt, to taste

ASSEMBLY

¼ cup Siberian sturgeon caviar,
for garnish

Charred onion Heat a skillet over high heat.
Add onions, place a weight on top (such as
another heavy pan, or a fish weight, or a burger
press), and cook without oil for 5 minutes, until
the bottom is completely charred.

Heat vinegar and butter in another skillet over
low heat. Add onion steaks, uncharred side
down, and braise for 20 to 30 minutes, until
tender but not disintegrating. Season to taste
with salt.

Assembly Fill a quarter of the tart shell with
warm vegetable demi. Place a warm charred
onion slice into each tart, spreading out the
onion to fill the tart's circumference. The demi
should fill the space between the onion and
the tart to the brim. Finish with a generous
quenelle of caviar.

WORMWOOD

▶ *NORTH PARK* ◀

CHEF / Trisha Vasquez

WORMWOOD, LOCATED on the North Park and University Heights border, is intimacy personified. The snug French bistro is all hexagon tiles, dim lighting, and cozy back garden patio. Here, executive chef Trisha Vasquez pushes the boundaries of French cuisine with southern Californian accents and nostalgic plays on elevated dishes sans the stuffiness of fine dining's past. For example, Wormwood's caviar cigar—made with masa crema, requesón, and avocado mousse and topped with caviar—is like "elevated finger food with the flavor profile of a street taco," Vasquez explains. The canapé reminds her of childhood and eating with her hands.

Growing up, food was a way to connect with her family. She cooked often with her dad and mom. Her grandma cooked a lot, too, and her grandpa was famous in the family for his BBQ. Vasquez spent her childhood watching the Food Network, taking art classes, and playing softball, so when she got older, the team-oriented nature of restaurants appealed to her. "Working hard and being on a team was bred in me," Vasquez says. Before Wormwood, Vasquez was pastry chef on the team at Jeune et Jolie that earned a Michelin star in 2021.

On the dinner plate, Vasquez's dishes echo the region's terroir, from southern California to Mexico. That might mean garnishing dishes with neon-colored nasturtiums in spring or serving a cacio e pepe with huitlacoche from Oaxaca. "I like to pay homage to our area while highlighting what's amazing about living in southern California," Vasquez says.

▶ *Sticky Toffee Gâteau with Brown Butter Ice Cream*

BROWN BUTTER ICE CREAM

⅔ cup (1⅓ sticks) butter

¼ cup nonfat milk powder

2 cups whole milk

2 cups heavy cream

1 tsp vanilla extract

1¼ cups sugar

½ tsp salt

13 egg yolks

GÂTEAU

Nonstick cooking spray

1 cup dried dates, pitted

½ tsp baking soda

¼ cup (½ stick) butter, room temperature

⅓ cup brown sugar

1 tsp salt

2 eggs

1 cup cake flour

2 tsp baking powder

STICKY SAUCE

½ cup brown sugar

2½ Tbsp heavy cream

2 tsp brandy

ASSEMBLY

Edible flowers, for garnish (optional)

Microgreens, for garnish (optional)

Sticky Toffee Gâteau with Brown Butter Ice Cream

SERVES
6–8

This delicious cake with dates and brandy syrup is—all at once—deep, rich, and warming. Top it off with a scoop of comfort, the brown butter ice cream. "Inspired by sticky toffee pudding, this dessert is like a warm hug," chef Trisha Vasquez says.

Brown butter ice cream Melt butter in a small saucepan over medium heat. Bring to a simmer and stir continuously until golden brown. Remove from heat, then whisk in milk powder. Transfer to a heatproof bowl and set aside.

In a small saucepan, combine milk, cream, vanilla, sugar, and salt. Simmer for 5 minutes, until sugar has completely dissolved. Remove pan from heat.

Whisk yolks in a separate bowl. Whisking continuously, add a third of the hot cream into the yolks. Whisk the yolk mixture back into the saucepan, then stir. Gently cook over medium-low heat, until it is thick enough to coat the back of a spoon or until the temperature reaches 170°F on an instant-read thermometer.

Strain through a fine-mesh sieve into a bowl. Whisk in brown butter mixture. Set aside to cool to room temperature. Cover, then chill in the refrigerator for at least 4 hours or overnight. Churn in an ice cream maker according to the manufacturer's instructions.

Gâteau Preheat oven to 350°F. Grease a six-count mini Bundt cake pan with nonstick cooking spray.

Combine dates and 1¼ cups of water in a saucepan. Bring to a boil over medium heat. Turn off heat, then immediately stir in baking soda. Transfer mixture to a high-powered blender and blend until smooth. Set aside to cool to room temperature.

In the bowl of a stand mixer fitted with the paddle attachment, combine butter, brown sugar, and salt and mix until smooth. Add eggs, one at a time, until fully incorporated.

In a separate bowl, sift together flour and baking powder. Add to the sugar mixture and mix until smooth. With the motor running on low speed, pour in the date mixture and mix until fully incorporated.

Pour the batter into the pan and bake for 20 minutes. Rotate pan and bake for another 15 to 20 minutes, until a toothpick comes out with only a few crumbs attached.

Sticky sauce Meanwhile, combine all ingredients in a small saucepan and bring to a simmer over medium heat. Whisk continuously until thickened.

Assembly Using a skewer, poke holes into the warm cake. Pour the warm sauce overtop, allowing it to fully soak in. Garnish with edible flowers and microgreens (if using). Serve warm with a scoop of ice cream.

1 lb cooked king crab legs

2 cups (4 sticks) butter (divided)

¼ cup cognac

1 tomato, chopped

2 large yellow onions, chopped (divided)

1 Tbsp thyme leaves

¼ cup light olive oil or avocado oil

3 leeks, thinly sliced

1 shallot, thinly sliced

2 cloves garlic, crushed

1 large russet potato, chopped

1 leaf hoja santa

¼ cup chopped spinach

1 Tbsp tarragon

Juice of 1 lemon

2 Tbsp salt, or to taste

½ cup crème fraîche, to serve

Potato chips, to serve

King Crab and Leek Soup
(Vichyssoise au Crabe)

SERVES
4–6

Chef Trisha Vasquez's southern Californian twist on classic potato leek soup calls for the bright Mexican herb hoja santa and finishes with a rich crab stock.

Soup With sharp kitchen shears, carefully cut open king crab legs while keeping meat intact. Remove meat and set aside. Rinse shells to remove any particles and dry on paper towels.

Melt ½ cup (1 stick) of butter in a large stockpot over medium-high heat, until it bubbles. Add crab shells and sauté for 3 minutes, until they turn a bright orange. Turn off heat, then deglaze pan with cognac, scraping up any bits on the bottom of the pan.

Add tomato and half of the onions and sauté over medium heat for 5 minutes, until onions are translucent. Add thyme and 2 quarts of water and bring to a boil. Cover, reduce to low heat, and simmer for an hour. Strain stock into a heatproof bowl and set aside.

Heat oil in a large saucepan over medium heat. Add leeks and the remaining onions and sauté for 7 minutes, until golden and translucent. Add shallot and garlic and sauté for a minute, stirring continuously to prevent garlic from burning.

Pour in crab stock, add potato, and simmer over medium heat for 30 minutes, until potato is fully cooked. Remove from heat. Stir in hoja santa, spinach, and tarragon.

Once the spinach is wilted, transfer mixture to a high-powered blender and blend until smooth. It should be a beautiful green color. Transfer soup back to the pan. Add ½ cup (1 stick) butter and lemon juice. Season to taste with salt.

Melt the remaining 1 cup (2 sticks) of butter in a small saucepan over medium heat. Add crab meat to warm through in the butter.

Top soup with crab meat and a dollop of crème fraîche, and enjoy with your favorite potato chips.

YOU & YOURS DISTILLING CO.

▶ *EAST VILLAGE* ◀

FOUNDER / Laura Johnson

GIN ENTHUSIASTS know to head to You & Yours Distilling Co.'s tasting room in downtown's East Village. They enter an airy space that feels like an industrial-chic living room with plush couches and potted and hanging plants dotted throughout. Concrete floors lead to a quartz bar where bottles of gin and vodka, distilled on site, line its shelves. Visitors sip on gin and vodka flights, socialize over cocktails like the Super-bloom—Y&Y's Citrus Vodka with grapefruit, basil, and a lavender sea salt rim—and fun snacks like house-made potato chips with green goddess ranch and spicy chicken bites drizzled in chili butter.

After college, founder Laura Johnson pivoted from pursuing wine education and noticed after visiting different distilleries that while other spirits like whiskey aged in barrels, the gins on offer seemed more of an after-thought. Plus, "The opportunities to introduce ingredients in unique ways, or to put your mark on the end product, just lit me up," Johnson, a self-described tinkerer, says of the distilling process.

Sensing an opportunity to approach gin differently, Johnson, with the help of her husband, Luke, opened You & Yours in 2017. Its flagship spirit, Sunday Gin, is the antithesis of the Christmas tree—flavored options on the market. It's floral, juicy, and bright. Juniper is still present, "but I use it more as a connective tissue to bring all of the other ingredients together and make them pop," Johnson says.

▶ *T-Bell Egg Rolls and Do You Want That Spicy? Cocktail*

EGG ROLLS

2 Tbsp chili powder

1 Tbsp ground cumin

1¼ tsp paprika

1¼ tsp salt

½ tsp pepper

½ tsp garlic powder

½ tsp onion powder

½ tsp dried oregano

1 lb ground beef

1 Tbsp olive oil

2 cups shredded Mexican cheese blend

6 egg roll wrappers

Vegetable oil, for frying

T-BELL HOT SAUCE

1 Tbsp vegetable oil

¾ cup tomato paste

1 tsp white vinegar

2 tsp chili powder

1½ tsp onion powder

1¼ tsp salt

1 tsp cayenne pepper

ASSEMBLY

Mexican crema, for garnish

1 thinly sliced purple radish, for garnish

Edible flowers, for garnish

Pinch of micro cilantro, for garnish

Lime wedges, to serve

T-Bell Egg Rolls

MAKES
6 egg rolls

Egg rolls Combine all spices in a large bowl. Add beef and gently mix until thoroughly combined.

Heat olive oil in a large skillet over medium-high heat. Add beef and sauté for 7 minutes. Fold in cheese, then drain excess oil. Set aside to cool.

Divide the filling into 6 portions. Spoon a portion of filling into an egg roll wrapper and fold according to package directions. Repeat with the remaining egg rolls.

Heat vegetable oil in a deep saucepan, until it reaches a temperature of 300°F. Gently lower egg rolls into the oil and fry for 3 minutes, or until browned all over. Work in batches, if needed, to avoid overcrowding. Using a slotted spoon, transfer to a paper towel–lined plate to drain. Set aside.

T-Bell hot sauce Heat oil in a saucepan over medium heat. Add tomato paste and cook for 2 to 3 minutes. Whisk in vinegar and 1½ cups of water.

Combine the remaining ingredients in a small bowl. Add the seasoning to the pan, then bring to a boil over high heat. Reduce heat to medium-low and simmer for 5 minutes. Remove from heat and set aside to cool.

Leftover hot sauce can be stored in an airtight container in the refrigerator for up to a week.

Assembly Place egg rolls on a plate and garnish with hot sauce, Mexican crema, radish, flowers, and micro cilantro. Serve with lime wedges.

GRAPEFRUIT CORDIAL

1 cup sugar

1 cup freshly squeezed
grapefruit juice

COCKTAIL

1½ oz You & Yours Sunday Gin

¾ oz Grapefruit Cordial (see here)

¾ oz cucumber juice

½ oz lime juice

Pinch of sea salt

1 to 4 dashes serrano bitters,
to taste (optional)

Ice

Sparkling water, such as Topo Chico

Cracked pink peppercorn, for garnish

Cucumber slice, for garnish

Do You Want That Spicy? Cocktail

SERVES

1

Grapefruit cordial Bring sugar and grapefruit juice to a boil in a saucepan. Stir until sugar has dissolved. Strain into a container and store tightly sealed in the refrigerator for up to a week.

Cocktail Combine gin, cordial, cucumber juice, lime juice, sea salt, and bitters (if using) in a cocktail shaker. Add ice and shake vigorously. Add a splash of sparkling water, then strain into a tall Collins glass filled with fresh ice.

Garnish with cracked pink peppercorn and a cucumber slice.

Metric Conversion Chart

VOLUME

IMPERIAL OR U.S.	→	METRIC
⅛ tsp	→	0.5 mL
¼ tsp	→	1 mL
½ tsp	→	2.5 mL
¾ tsp	→	4 mL
1 tsp	→	5 mL
½ Tbsp	→	8 mL
1 Tbsp	→	15 mL
1½ Tbsp	→	23 mL
2 Tbsp	→	30 mL
¼ cup	→	60 mL
⅓ cup	→	80 mL
½ cup	→	125 mL
⅔ cup	→	165 mL
¾ cup	→	185 mL
1 cup	→	250 mL
1¼ cups	→	310 mL
1⅓ cups	→	330 mL
1½ cups	→	375 mL
1⅔ cups	→	415 mL
1¾ cups	→	435 mL
2 cups	→	500 mL
2¼ cups	→	560 mL
2⅓ cups	→	580 mL
2½ cups	→	625 mL
2¾ cups	→	690 mL
3 cups	→	750 mL
4 cups / 1 quart	→	1 L
5 cups	→	1.25 L
6 cups	→	1.5 L
7 cups	→	1.75 L
8 cups	→	2 L
12 cups	→	3 L

LIQUID MEASURES
(FOR ALCOHOL)

IMPERIAL OR U.S.	→	METRIC
½ fl oz	→	15 mL
1 fl oz	→	30 mL
2 fl oz	→	60 mL
3 fl oz	→	90 mL
4 fl oz	→	120 mL

CANS AND JARS

IMPERIAL OR U.S.	→	METRIC
6 oz	→	170 g
14 oz	→	398 mL
19 oz	→	540 mL
28 oz	→	796 mL

WEIGHT

IMPERIAL OR U.S.	→	METRIC
½ oz	→	15 g
1 oz	→	30 g
2 oz	→	60 g
3 oz	→	85 g
4 oz (¼ lb)	→	115 g
5 oz	→	140 g
6 oz	→	170 g
7 oz	→	200 g
8 oz (½ lb)	→	225 g
9 oz	→	255 g
10 oz	→	285 g
11 oz	→	310 g
12 oz (¾ lb)	→	340 g
13 oz	→	370 g
14 oz	→	400 g
15 oz	→	425 g
16 oz (1 lb)	→	450 g
1¼ lbs	→	570 g
1½ lbs	→	670 g
2 lbs	→	900 g
3 lbs	→	1.4 kg
4 lbs	→	1.8 kg
5 lbs	→	2.3 kg
6 lbs	→	2.7 kg

LINEAR

IMPERIAL OR U.S.		METRIC
⅛ inch	→	3 mm
¼ inch	→	6 mm
½ inch	→	12 mm
¾ inch	→	2 cm
1 inch	→	2.5 cm
1¼ inches	→	3 cm
1½ inches	→	3.5 cm
1¾ inches	→	4.5 cm
2 inches	→	5 cm
2½ inches	→	6.5 cm
3 inches	→	7.5 cm
4 inches	→	10 cm
5 inches	→	12.5 cm
6 inches	→	15 cm
7 inches	→	18 cm
10 inches	→	25 cm
12 inches (1 foot)	→	30 cm
13 inches	→	33 cm
16 inches	→	41 cm
18 inches	→	46 cm
24 inches (2 feet)	→	60 cm
28 inches	→	70 cm
30 inches	→	75 cm
6 feet	→	1.8 m

TEMPERATURE
(FOR OVEN TEMPERATURES, SEE CHART IN NEXT COLUMN)

IMPERIAL OR U.S.		METRIC
90°F	→	32°C
120°F	→	49°C
125°F	→	52°C
130°F	→	54°C
140°F	→	60°C
150°F	→	66°C
155°F	→	68°C
160°F	→	71°C
165°F	→	74°C
170°F	→	77°C
175°F	→	80°C
180°F	→	82°C
190°F	→	88°C
200°F	→	93°C
240°F	→	116°C
250°F	→	121°C
300°F	→	149°C
325°F	→	163°C
350°F	→	177°C
360°F	→	182°C
375°F	→	191°C

OVEN TEMPERATURE

IMPERIAL OR U.S.		METRIC
200°F	→	95°C
250°F	→	120°C
275°F	→	135°C
300°F	→	150°C
325°F	→	160°C
350°F	→	180°C
375°F	→	190°C
400°F	→	200°C
425°F	→	220°C
450°F	→	230°C
500°F	→	260°C
550°F	→	290°C

BAKING PANS

IMPERIAL OR U.S.		METRIC
5- × 9-inch loaf pan	→	2 L loaf pan
9- × 13-inch cake pan	→	4 L cake pan
11- × 17-inch baking sheet	→	30 × 45 cm baking sheet

Acknowledgments

THANK YOU to Deanna—colleague, friend, therapist, the big sister I didn't know I wanted. We made a book! I couldn't have done it without you. Thank you also to Taylor and Keith for making the food look beautiful for Dee's lens. To Marcus, Yannikins, Sami, Shannon, Melina, Ryan, Nicole, thank you for your fierce support and encouragement. Your presence has buoyed me for years, and through this project, no exception. And thank you to the Figure 1 team, our patience and persistence have paid off. This project began in 2019, halted abruptly in 2020, sputtered back to life in 2022, and found its footing in 2023. *San Diego Cooks* is a case study in resilience, and a delicious one at that.

Index

LIGAYA MALONES is a San Diego–based writer who covers food, travel, and culture. She has written for numerous publications and websites, including *New York* magazine, *San Diego Magazine*, *Condé Nast Traveler*, Food52, *Bon Appétit*, Lonely Planet, and Eater. *San Diego Cooks* is her first book.

DEANNA SANDOVAL is a San Diego–based food and lifestyle photographer. Her bold, vibrant, and playful photographs have appeared in regional and national publications and websites, including *Wine Enthusiast*, *San Diego Magazine*, The Infatuation, and *Edible San Diego.* In 2015, she launched Smoke & Brine, a food events and catering business. *San Diego Cooks* is her first book.

ABOUT THE AUTHORS

▶ *SAN DIEGO* ◀

AUTHOR (L) Ligaya Malones

PHOTOGRAPHER (R) Deanna Sandoval